A COMMERCIAL DREAM

Herbert, Cardinal Vaughan
2nd Bishop of Salford 1872-1892
3rd Archbishop of Westminster 1892-1903

FOUNDER OF ST BEDE'S COLLEGE

A History of St Bede's College Manchester

Volume 1
A Commercial Dream - 1876-1891

Lawrence R. Gregory

First published in 2014

By The Salford Diocesan Archives

St Augustine's, Grosvenor Square, Manchester

TABLE OF CONTENTS

LIST OF ILLUSTRATIONS

ACKNOWLEDGMENTS

The completion of this project would not have been possible without the patience and cooperation of several people; at St Bede's my primary thanks go to the College Librarian Karen Poolton who has accommodated my numerous requests for access to the archives, also to Fr Tony Dearman who has allowed me to repeatedly pick his encyclopaedic memory and thus provided much useful information and who has also proof-read various drafts, and not least the present headmaster Daniel Kearney who as my Sixth Form Tutor and mentor greatly encouraged me to pursue my interest in College history. My fellow Old Bedian and lifelong friend Mr Thomas Robson, now Classics Master at the Ipswich School, has helped me with translations.

My colleagues at the Salford Diocesan Archives, Dr David Lannon, Dr John Broadley and Fr Nicholas Paxton, have also provided much guidance and assistance, and information has been forthcoming from, Mr Jonathan Bush at Ushaw, Fr Sullivan at Westminster, Meg Whittle at Liverpool, David Kay at St Edmund's College, Ware, Kevin Cawley at Notre Dame University, USA, Sister Shelia Tate of the Cenacle Sisters, David Knight and Margaret Panikkar at Stonyhurst, Anna Edwards at Farm Street and finally Fr O'Brien MHM, archivist of the Mill Hill Missionaries.

DEDICATION

To the memory of Mrs Lynne Harter who inspired a love of history among countless generations of Bedians.

INTRODUCTION

During thc 20th century, St Bede's College, Manchester would attain a position as one of the leading Catholic secondary schools in the United Kingdom; the first official HMI inspection following the approval of St Bede's for government grants, took place in 1923 and described the school as an "Excellent Classical College". Yet this was totally inconsistent with the intentions of Bishop Herbert Vaughan when he first conceived of the institution fifty years earlier in 1872; Vaughan had been quite clear that St Bede's was to be a Commercial Business College and even went so far as to exclude Latin and Greek from the syllabus entirely. However following a merger with the Diocesan Classical College and Junior Seminary, the Salford Catholic Grammar School, in 1891, the latter institution engulfed and swamped the former.

No real and accurate account of the history of St Bede's College has ever been published, certainly not one which gives a clear picture of events during the sixteen year history of the commercial school, and although there are brief accounts appearing here and there, these generally gloss over the details of the rise and fall of Vaughan's ambitious experiment. The first and arguably most accurate attempt to chronicle the College progress was written by an unknown author in 1902 and was first published in the 1903 Salford Diocesan Almanac, then later as a small booklet entitled 'St Bede's College – A Brief Historical Sketch'. Seven years later, and six years after the death of its subject, John Snead-Cox published his two-volume 'Life of Cardinal Vaughan'. Snead-Cox was Vaughan's cousin and the biography presents a somewhat biased and rose-tinted view of the Cardinal's career. Within the first Volume can be found an entire chapter on the establishment of the Commercial College and although this contains some useful and entertaining anecdotes, it is en masse historically inaccurate and Louis Charles Casartelli, then in the seventh year of his episcopate, actually wrote to the author at the time to point this out and requested that corrections be made prior to publication of the 2nd edition[1] – a 2nd edition was never released. Most significantly the chapter on the College is concluded with the statement that "Before leaving Salford the Bishop was able to incorporate the Salford Grammar School with the now flourishing foundation at St Bede's[2]".

[1] SDA157, Pg 769, Casartelli to Cox, 20/6/1910.
[2] SNEAD-COX, J., 1910, *The Life of Cardinal Vaughan*, vol. 1, p. 319.

The next historian to attempt to broach the subject of Bedian history was school master and sometime librarian Wilfred Whalley[1], who in his 1938 M.Ed thesis 'A Historical Account of Catholic Education in England: with special reference to Educational Activities in the Salford Diocese', wrote much on St Bede's and was also probably responsible for a series of potted histories in Baeda in the 1920s and 30s. Unfortunately by this point, the Snead-Coxian view of the history had taken root and would colour everything written after, including to some extent the two subsequent biographies of Vaughan. In fact it was not until the last ten years that the first attempt to write more accurate accounts was undertaken by Dr John Broadley in his two books, 'A Bishop in Peace & War: The Life of Louis Charles Casartelli'; and 'Bishop Vaughan & the Jesuits'.

Having read everything that had been written on St Bede's, the two most important points left unanswered in my opinion were, if the Commercial College was in 1891 'flourishing' as Snead-Cox puts it, then why was it forced to merge with the Grammar School, a school which later consumed it, and secondly why was the grand College building never completed?

My involvement with the College began in the early 1990s as a nine-year-old primary school pupil and would continue for the next nine years; during this time I found myself captivated by the history of the place and spent many hours ensconced in the upper floor of the Library browsing and attempting to understand the archives held there. After leaving Sixth Form I became involved with the Salford Diocesan Archives and thus was able to develop my research into the school; it soon became apparent that if I was to truly explain and understand the real history of the brief sixteen-year existence of the Commercial College, then it would be necessary to disregard most of the secondary sources, and instead locate and collate, where possible, original records.

Vaughan left very few archives, destroying many of his personal papers prior to his death[2]. What had survived is held either in Westminster or by the Mill Hill Missionaries, with Salford possessing only copies of his Acta; however his friend and regular correspondent Lady Herbert of Lea had meticulously kept every letter she received from him, and these were published in 1942 by Burns & Oates, edited by Shane Leslie; Bishop Casartelli had also kept the letters he'd received from Vaughan, which in addition to his personal diaries provide a valuable collection; these are held between the Salford Diocese and Ushaw College. At St Bede's, the College Log Books were extant, albeit with a ten-year gap (1881-1891), as are the College Admission Registers (1876-1991), back copies of the College Magazines and a small quantity of administrative papers, preserved by that venerable College institution, Fr Bernard Jackson (1911-2005), whom I had the privilege to interview in 2004. The local, Catholic and National Press from the era also provided a useful resource as an

---

[1] Wilfred 'Bill' Whalley (1902-1978), on staff from 1925 teaching history, then English, then Geography. After retirement became College Librarian.

[2] McCORMACK MHM, A., 1966, *Cardinal Vaughan*, London, p. 338

‘outsider’s view’ of events. It was thus possible to build up what I hope to be the first accurate picture of the sixteen-year history of the St Bede’s Commercial College.

Part One
Catholic Education
Up to 1876

Bishop William Turner
4th Rector of Rook Street 1835-1842
3rd Rector of Granby Row 1842-1853
1st Bishop of Salford 1850-1872

Pre-Diocesan Education

To fully understand the situation surrounding the establishment of St Bede's College in January 1876 it is necessary to first understand the Catholic educational situation in Manchester & Salford at the time of Herbert Vaughan's elevation to the episcopate and to the See of Salford in 1872.

The area of Lancashire that would form the new Diocese in 1850 covered the historic Hundreds of Blackburn and Salford and although it stretched as far as the Ribble Valley in the North, the primary population was centred at the southernmost region in the twin towns of Manchester and Salford. The towns were served in 1850 by seven Catholic Missions; St Chad's was the mother church which in 1847 was relocated from Rook Street (near Market Street) to a new church on Cheetham Hill; from St Chad's was opened St Mary, Mulberry Street in 1794 (rebuilt on the same site in 1848); St Augustine's was opened on Granby Row in 1820 as an intended replacement of the Rook Street Chapel; St Patrick's was opened on Livesey Street in 1832, St Wilfrid's, Hulme in 1842 and finally St Anne's, Ancoats in 1848. On the west side of the River Irwell, St John's, Salford (later the Cathedral) was also opened in 1848.

In 1836, a survey was taken of Sunday Schools in Manchester & Salford and it listed the following institutions as being run by the Catholic Church, along with the numbers of pupils in attendance; Livesey Street had schools at Sycamore Street, Oldham Road (231), George Leigh Street, Oldham Road (350), Dyche Street, Angel Meadow (1050) and Newton Heath (75). Granby Row meanwhile had two: its own school under the church (900) and Little Ireland (555). Finally Mulberry Street ran Lloyd Street (site of Albert Square), (415), Green Street, Hulme (104), Bury Street, Salford (500) and Charlestown (115)[1]. This made a total of 4295 children attending Catholic Sunday School in 1836.

The development of Catholic Elementary Schools was much slower and appeared to have been commenced by the Christian Brothers under Brother Francis Phelan[2] who came to Manchester from Dublin in 1838. They initially took charge of the Lloyd Street School, which was converted from a Sunday School into Manchester's first Catholic Day School, then in 1845 moved to take over the Livesey Street Boys' Schools[3]; there the Girls' School had been opened by the Presentation Sisters in 1836 and the Boys' School under a lay master in 1838[4]. In 1844 a two-storey school building was opened at Salford, which would later be attached to the Cathedral Mission; here the boys were taught on the ground floor by the Christian Brothers and the girls' school was later opened on the upper floor in 1847 by the Daughters of

[1] O'DEA, J., 1910, *The Story of the Old Faith in Manchester*, p. 215
[2] Brother Phelan retired back to Dublin from Manchester and died there in December 1868.
[3] O'DEA, J., 1910, *The Story of the Old Faith in Manchester*, p. 217
[4] ANON., 1927, *History of St Patrick's RC Club*, p. 56-58

Charity of SVP. These were the only three Catholic Elementary schools in Manchester & Salford at the time of the establishment of the new Diocese in 1850.

The Xaverian Brothers in Manchester

The Xaverian Congregation had been founded by T.J. Ryken in Bruges, Belgium, in 1845 and first came to England in April 1848. Father James Peacock, the Rector of St Marie's Church, Bury, had made initial contact with Ryken in 1846 and in August the following year a letter was sent detailing their requirements, and the three Brothers arrived on the 29th April 1848; Br Alphonsus (Superior), Br Ignatius (Musician) and Br Alexius (Domestic). In July 1849, Br Alphonsus was recalled to Belgium and Br Ignatius was appointed superior in his place. Br Stanislaus Lucas was then sent to Bury as the third member of the Community[1].

The initial two-year contract at Bury was due to expire on the 1st May 1850. Fr Peacock had been suffering from ill health since early 1849 and had moved to reside at Holcombe with the hope that the fresh air would restore him. It was unsuccessful however and in November 1849 he resigned his Mission, and the newly ordained Fr Thomas Allen was then appointed to take charge on a temporary basis. Devadder states that when Fr Peacock left Bury, Fr Allen placed St Marie's School under Government Examination and that the Xaverians were not yet qualified to undertake this and this then forced their removal from the town; however letters between Ryken and Peacock suggest that the Mission was also unable to financially support the brothers for another year[2].

Ryken had been contacted in January 1850 by Fr Peter Benoit, curate at Granby Row, requesting the presence of the Congregation to establish a school for his Mission, and in March, following the developments at Bury, Ryken wrote back to advise that Brothers Ignatius, Alexius and Stanislaus would move to Manchester the following month. The Brothers initially took up residence at 6 Bedford Street, Hulme[3].

At the end of April 1850, Fr William Turner, the Rector at Granby Row, released a flier to his congregation: "The parents of children residing in this district are informed that on the 1st May 1850, the Boys School will be opened by a Community of Religious Brothers". With no appropriate space available for the teaching to be undertaken, the Brothers were forced to open the school in the burial crypt of the church[4] and an unidentified contemporary Xaverian source described the situation thus:

> "The school was at this time in the poorest condition possible – located under the church, and surrounded by tombs, it resembled an immense vault, dark and

[1] DEVADDER, J., *The Life & Times of TJ Ryken*, vol. 2, p. 121-122
[2] Ibid, p.147
[3] Ibid, p. 149-150
[4] This was a separate section of the church under-croft from the existing Sunday-Schoolroom.

> dismal in the extreme. In addition to the darkness, the surrounding graves gave forth so unsupportable a stench that the place became almost unbearable... The school furniture and appliances were of a most meagre description, yet, notwithstanding these disadvantages the number of scholars rapidly increased...[1]"

The fact that the Catholic parents were still prepared to send their sons to be educated there despite such conditions demonstrates the urgent requirement that existed for the provision of Catholic education in Manchester at the time.

In July 1852, the then Canon Benoit opened a chapel-of-ease at Ardwick in a disused factory on Ogden Street; the new Mission was dedicated to St Aloysius and the school was opened under the Brothers; with Br Joseph Geoghegan[2] sent to England to run it with Br John Segers. With the increased numbers in their Community the brothers moved to a larger residence at 64 Grosvenor Street.

> "In England... where our brothers are extremely well liked by the bishop and the clergy... there are about 370 children in our school; a second school has just recently been opened and we hope that it will soon surpass the first one[3]".

In March 1853 the St Augustine's School in the crypt was forced to shut and the boys transferred to Ardwick which then became the main school. "Through this merger the Ardwick school became a big institution with five brothers and over 400 students[4]". In 1854 work then commenced at Granby Row to construct the first purpose built Catholic elementary school in Manchester, the site being at the rear of the church on a portion of the former grave-yard[5]. The school was opened in 1855 with the elementary age boys and girls sharing the new building while the infant classes continued to be undertaken in the Sunday Schoolroom under the church.

Educational Growth under Bishop Turner

Fr William Turner was elected 1st Bishop of Salford on the 22nd June 1851 and was consecrated on the 25th July; he initially remained at Granby Row, due to the lack of an episcopal residence. One of his first priorities was the development of elementary education provision in his new Diocese and over the next two decades a network of new schools were opened across inner-city Manchester, many utilising the existing Sunday School premises: St Wilfrid's (1851), St Chad's (1851), St Alphonsus Infants, Chorlton on Medlock (1856), St Aloysius, Ardwick (1856), St Joseph, Goulden Street (1863), St Alban, Fawcett St, Ancoats (1863), St Anne, Ancoats (1865), St William, Dyche St, Angel Meadow (1865), and St Edward, Rusholme (1866).

---

[1] DEVADDER, J., *The Life & Times of TJ Ryken*, vol. 2, p. 185.
[2] The 4th member of the community and the first Irish brother.
[3] DEVADDER, J., *The Life & Times of TJ Ryken*, vol. 2, p. 192.
[4] Ibid, p. 192.
[5] Manchester Guardian, 5/7/1854, p. 5

In April 1857, the Christian Brothers resigned from the Cathedral Schools and the Xaverians stepped in to take them over. Consequently Brother Ryken increased the numbers in the Manchester community to six: three formed the staff at Granby Row, while three took over the staff at the Cathedral[1]. Two years later the brothers also took charge at St Chad's: "In January 1859... [we took] charge of St Chad's Dayschool which was our first school under Government inspection... The brothers had now charge of the three principal Catholic schools in Manchester and Salford... [and]... the Community of the Manchester House had now increased to eight members[2]". By the end of 1859 there were ten brothers in the Manchester Community, running three elementary schools. This arrangement would continue until the 1880s when they would gradually surrender control of the schools, the final one being St Augustine's which they left in January 1888; this was in order that they could focus their efforts on secondary education.

Secondary Education

In spring 1852, Canon Benoit first proposed to Brother Ryken that he should open a Catholic Middle School in Manchester. He suggested that Br Alphonsus be sent back to England to run it and that the proceeds be used to support St Augustine's parish work. Ryken was upset about what he saw as Benoit's attempts to interfere in the running of the Congregation and stated that if a secondary and boarding school was to be opened it was to be run for the benefit of the Xaverians themselves[3]. Despite the disagreements, in January 1853 Br Paul Van Gerwen[4] opened a 'Middle Day-School' at the Xaverian residence in Grosvenor St[5]. However within a couple of months of the opening of the Xaverian College, news was spread that the Jesuit Fathers had also been given permission to establish a Middle School in Manchester and that Fr Jerrard Strickland SJ had acquired a property called 'Bloomsbury' on Granby Row, with the intention of opening it there. Ryken reacted badly to the news of the development and on the 23rd February wrote an angry letter to Benoit:

> Reverend Father, I learned that the Jesuits will establish a middle-class school in Manchester, namely in Granby Row. I am really shocked and these are the reasons why, you had more or less agreed that we would start a Middle-Class school at the beginning of the summer and I have not heard even with a single word about the Jesuits coming and had not been asked whether [the Xaverians] were able to make the projected start or not. Now all my plans for Manchester are jeopardised... and this after all the sacrifices we made for the parish of St Augustine's... since you do not want to postpone your plan (for the Jesuits) any

[1] DEVADDER, J., *The Life & Times of TJ Ryken*, vol. 2, p. 354.
[2] Ibid, p. 402. (Memoirs of Br John Segers)
[3] Ibid, p. 191.
[4] Br Paul first came to Manchester in 1850 but only stayed for a few weeks; he then came back in July 1852 to replace Br Alexis.
[5] DEVADDER, J., *The Life & Times of TJ Ryken*, vol. 2, p. 231.

> longer, we have no other choice than let it have its course and leave Manchester in due time – a thing which I have decided to do in this case[1]".

The Xaverian School closed in December 1853 and true to his word Ryken began to gradually pull the Congregation out of Manchester; Brothers Paul and Ignatius left for America in April 1854 and by December of that year only two members of the Community were left in the town; John Segers and Stanislaus Lucas. Devadder does however question "whether the Xaverian Brothers were qualified in 1853 to staff an English speaking school at secondary level[2]".

The Catholic Collegiate Institute

The Jesuit Fathers arrived in Manchester in mid-1853 and opened their new school in September of that same year. The original staff consisted of one priest, Fr Jerrard Strickland[3], one scholastic, T. Parkinson, and a lay brother[4]. It would seem that initial development was slow and the school failed to return the results that Strickland had hoped for and on the 20th May 1854, after only eighteen months in Manchester, they wrote to Bishop Turner to advise that they were leaving the town. Turner replied to the Jesuit Superior:

> "I am in receipt of your communication and regret exceedingly that you should consider it your duty to abandon the school in Manchester and withdraw Fr Strickland. The experiment made has, I confess surpassed my expectations. On referring to a copy of a letter to Fr Etheridge I then informed him that I could not calculate on having more than about 30 scholars. There are now 52 boys. This encourages me to hope that the numbers will gradually increase. Aware of the consequences of breaking up the school, now so happily begun, it is my intention to carry it on and place at the head of it one of my clergy. To Fr. Strickland, I am under many obligations for his praiseworthy exertions; he has, I conceive, done a real service to religion. To yourself and to the Fathers of the Society I owe a debt of gratitude for the kindness and courtesy that I have received. It shall be my study to keep up and maintain that cordiality and harmony which ought to exist between a Bishop and the Society[5]".

Vaughan would later describe the 1854 departure as the Jesuits "throwing the remains of their undertaking upon the late Bishop[6]". He also claimed that the Order had promised to invest £5000 in the new school, but failed to do so. The Jesuits meanwhile claimed that their departure was due to their being not allowed to open a

---

[1] Ibid, p. 232.
[2] DEVADDER, J., *The Life & Times of TJ Ryken*, vol. 2, p.
[3] Fr Strickland was educated at Downside; after leaving Manchester he served at Accrington for two years before making his name as a chaplain in the Crimea working alongside Fr Sidney Woolett. He died on duty on the 26th April 1856 from an illness contracted attending to soldiers in a field hospital.
[4] RAFFERTY, O.P., *The English Jesuit College Manchester 1875*, Recusant History, vol. 20.2, p. 292-93.
[5] BROADLEY, J., 2010, *Bishop Vaughan & the Jesuits*, Pg 7, (Turner to Joseph Johnson).
[6] Ibid, appendix 3, (Vaughan to his agent in Rome, 20/12/1874).

Mission Church attached to the school, which made their position untenable. Fr Gallwey claimed in August 1874 that "had we any hope left of being allowed a church, we would certainly have held our ground[1]".

Due to their decreased numbers in 1854, the Manchester Xaverians were now in no position to take over the Secondary School and as a result Bishop Turner was forced to run it under the charge of his own Diocesan Clergy. Fr Peter Vermeulen, curate at St Chad's, was sent as first secular Headmaster and classes were relocated from Granby Row to a large detached house on Lower Ormond St, Grosvenor Square. The school appears for the first time in the Catholic Directory of England and Wales in 1855 (compiled at the latter end of 1854); Vermeulen was removed to Ancoats after barely a year and was replaced by Fr Henry Browne, curate at Mulberry St. Fr Browne ran the school until 1858 when he was sent to Levenshulme[2]. The final secular priest to serve as Headmaster was Fr Adrian de Smeth, a Belgian who did not appear to be affiliated to the Diocese, and with the exception of his two years at the Institute no record can be found of him.

The 1861 Census of England and Wales records the Collegiate Institute extant at 46 Ormond Street, with two resident staff, Fr de Smet (sic) and Daniel Louis Minahan. In addition there are two female servants and three male boarders, Thomas Quick[3] and Alfred & Jules Ferez from France[4]. The history of the Xaverian College, Manchester suggests that for a short period, the school was under the management of a lay-master[5], but it is not clear where this idea comes from; one possibility is that de Smeth was recalled to Belgium and Minahan was left in charge by proxy. What we do know is that in August 1862, the Diocese withdrew and charge of the Collegiate Institute was entrusted into the care of the Xaverian Brothers, who within a few years considerably extended the buildings and facilities:

> "The Roman Catholic Collegiate Institute stands in Grosvenor-Square; was considerably extended in 1866; and includes, in the new parts alone, a dining-hall 50 feet long, new class-rooms, a library, a chapel, a refectory, seventeen dormitories, and a covered play-ground[6]".

The exact reasons why Turner decided in 1862 to surrender control of the Collegiate Institute are not recorded. Devadder suggests that the Institute was failing under the Diocese and was at the point of closure and this is echoed by Lannon[7] and by Rafferty, the latter who states that "the plight of the school had become so acute

---

[1] BROADLEY, J., 2010, *Bishop Vaughan & the Jesuits*, p. 7, (Gallwey to Vaughan, 20/8/1874).
[2] CROFT & GILLOW, 1902, *Historical Account of Lisbon College*, p.183.
[3] The annals of the Diocese record Fr Thomas Quick (1833-1898), who was ordained in 1863. It is not clear if this is the same man.
[4] Census of England & Wales, Chorlton on Medlock Civil Parish, Folio 53, p. 8, 7/4/1861.
[5] ANON, 2012, *History of Xaverian College.*
[6] WILSON, J.M., 1870, *Imperial Gazetter of England & Wales.*
[7] LANNON, D., 1993, Unpublished thesis.

owing to the shortage of staff and money[1]". But the evidence for this statement is unclear and it is somewhat undermined by the fact that almost immediately Turner gives up the Institute, he opens a new Grammar School in Salford, and when the Bishop announces this decision to the Diocese, his criticism of the Institute is clear:

> "We have, on a former occasion communicated to you our views concerning the education of our youth of the Middle Classes of Society… we opened the Catholic Institute, which has been in active operation for upwards of eight years. With the general results of that school we see no reason to be dissatisfied. At present, however, the youth of the Middle Class aspire to a higher standard of education than what was afforded by the teachers of the Catholic Institute. In order to supply this want, we have resolved to form a Grammar School of our own, adjoining our residence that shall be under our immediate superintendence, and where the advantages of a good commercial and religious education will be combined[2]".

Turner's attitude here is that the Diocese requires a higher grade of Classical education for the Middle Classes, which is not being provided at the Institute. In some ways Turner feeling the need to establish a new school is quite a damning critique of the Institute.

The Salford Catholic Grammar School

Bishop Turner had moved out of Granby Row in August 1853 to take up residence on The Crescent, Salford[3] and the Salford Catholic Grammar School was opened there in May 1862. Fr Augustus de Clerc[4] was appointed President with Fr Henry Beswick[5] as Vice-President. School fees were one guinea per quarter; books and stationery were extra; "the course of studies will comprise all the branches of a classical education, viz:- Latin, Greek, English and French; Arithmetic and Mathematics; Bookkeeping, the elements of Natural Philosophy, vocal music and drawing[6]". It was stated that boys were admissible as soon as they were able to read.

Among the first day's intake was the eleven year old Louis Charles Casartelli, a second generation Italian immigrant and son of a prominent Manchester chemist and instrument maker. Following ordination in 1876 Casartelli would play an important role in the history of St Bede's College, serving periods as Prefect of Studies, Rector and then later Bishop of Salford. He recorded his recollections of the early days of the SCGS in a memoir written for Baeda in commemoration of the Golden Jubilee:

---

[1] RAFFERTY, O.P., *The English Jesuit College Manchester 1875*, Recusant History, vol. 20.2, p. 293.
[2] TURNER, Bp W., *Letter to the Catholics of Manchester & Salford*, 1/3/1862.
[3] The Tablet, 13/08/1853, p. 4.
[4] Mgr Augustus Joseph de Clerc (1831-1889 – Ord 1856). Born in Bruges.
[5] Fr Henry Beswick (1832-1880 – Ord 1862). Assistant at Cathedral and on staff at the SCGS. Appointed Rector at Greengate in 1868, where he died.
[6] TURNER, Bp W., *Letter to the Catholics of Manchester & Salford*, 1/3/1862.

> "A bright sunny May Day morning, exactly fifty years ago. A little boy... was hurrying down the Crescent, Salford... turning the corner of the solidly built house then numbered 24, making his way down the broad passage that divided it from its neighbour and led to the stables at the back... and so at 9am the new school began with six pupils. Fr De Clerc, whose name is still held in veneration by hundreds, then a young priest of thirty, received us and began to test our knowledge. His method was ingenious: he gave us each a sheet of foolscap, dictated the names of all the books we should need for lessons, with their respective prices, and then bade us to add up the total. Thus we had an examination in handwriting, spelling and arithmetic all in one!... At the time our playground was really the Bishop's garden, and a fine garden it was, with lawns and beautiful flower-beds. Perhaps it is hardly necessary to state that before many months were out, grass and flower-beds had disappeared. And the school-house itself? As said above, it consisted just of the stables of the Bishop's House, refitted so as to make a fairly presentable large school-room. At first only the big room downstairs was used; later the haylofts upstairs were transformed and good classrooms created... So good old Bishop Turner, with his clergy, went on living in the fine roomy Bishop's House, which later on was the boarding-school... Although we began the school with only six boys on the first day, the numbers speedily increased, during the three months, or so, of our first academic year... up to Sept 1864 the school was only a day school. At that date Bishop Turner and his Secretary, Canon Benoit[1], withdrew to 2 Marlborough Terrace, Peel Park and his former house was given over to the staff and boarders[2]".

It would seem apparent that the new College enjoyed early and almost immediate success and by the end of the first Academic Year a very favourable report was published in the Catholic press:

> The first annual Exhibition of the Catholic Grammar School under the immediate patronage of the Lord Bishop of Salford, took place on Friday July 31st, in the Lecture Hall of the Young Men's Society, and was a very great success. The pupils acquitted themselves in the higher branches of their Educational course with much ability and merited not only the eulogiums passed upon them, but the premiums awarded for their assiduity[3]".

[1] Canon Benoit had left Granby Row with Bishop Turner in 1853 and would remain as Bishop's Secretary until the latter's death in 1872, at which time Vaughan sent him as Rector of Mill Hill, where he died in 1892.

[2] BAEDA, New Vol 1.6, May 1912, p. 184-7, (Memoir of Bishop Casartelli).

[3] THE TABLET, 15/8/1863, p. 7.

Fr Bruno de Splenter[1] joined the staff in 1864 and in 1866 Mr G. Chapman was employed as the first lay-master. The school expanded rapidly and in 1880 the adjoining house at 22 The Crescent was purchased and the two buildings connected together[2]. In April 1887, the famous SCGS Literary Society was formed by Fr de Splenter and Fr J. Mills, with a young student, Mr Anselm Poock[3] as first secretary[4]. Mgr de Clerc would remain in charge until his death in 1889, when he was replaced briefly by Fr John Bromley Cooke and at the time of the 1891 merger, the staff at the SCGS numbered eight, four clergy and four laymen.

St Chad's High School

The Xaverians in the late 1870s attempted to establish a second High School, using the school buildings at St Chad's. Little is known about it, beyond the following description which appeared in an advert in 1878:

> "Built under the very shadow of the Church, on land adjoining the Rectory, and commanding a view of Cheetham Hill Road, St Chad's High School, consisting of two spacious well-ventilated and cheerful rooms, will compare favourably with any school of the kind in Manchester, in point of position of completeness and fitness for the purpose of education. The course of studies comprises the usual branches of an English and Commercial Education. The study of the French language… a practical knowledge of drawing…[5]"

The St Chad's High School seems to have ceased operation in the early 1890s and several of its pupils joined St Bede's at the time of the merger with the Salford Catholic Grammar School[6].

The Arrival of Herbert Vaughan

Bishop Turner died on the 12th July 1872 and his replacement, Herbert Vaughan, was at the time running his recently established Missionary College at Mill Hill in the Archdiocese of Westminster; he was appointed to Salford on the 27th September and consecrated on the 28th October. Canon Benoit, who had been tipped as a potential replacement for Turner, was sent by Vaughan to take charge at Mill Hill. Just over a month after his consecration Vaughan wrote a letter to Canon Kershaw[7] which was

---

[1] Canon Bruno de Splenter (1835-1899 – Ord 1862) born in Belgium and joined the Salford Diocese in 1864 and on non-residential staff at SCGS and Pastoral Seminary until 1880. In 1876 founded St Edmund, Miles Platting, where he remained until retirement in 1898.
[2] Salford Diocese Finance Board, Minute Book, vol. 1, p. 145, 7/4/1880.
[3] Mgr Anselm Poock (1864-1926 – Ord. 1896). Old boy of the SCGS. Joined staff at St Bede's in 1900 as 4th Procurator, then 4th Rector 1903. In 1912 went as Rector to St Augustine's, Manchester where he died.
[4] FRONDES SILVULAE, vol. II, no. 33, June 1887, p. 122.
[5] SALFORD DIOCESAN ALMANAC, 1878, Pg 53.
[6] St Bede's College, Admission registers, vol. 2.
[7] Mgr Canon John Kershaw (1816-1890, ord. - 1843), Rector at All Saints, Barton (1845-1890).

distributed to all Priests and Missions in the Diocese, outlining his plans for Catholic Education in Manchester & Salford.

> "...it would be in the highest spiritual interest alike to establish a seminary of Pastoral Theology within the diocese, in which all students who had finished their third year of theology elsewhere should enter for at least one year. During that time they would live with the Bishop and become known to him, and to the clergy and to one another... Suitable provision has yet to be made for the education of a higher class, so that the next Diocesan undertaking, after the work of the Seminary, must be to carry on to completion the work of the Grammar School, prudently and wisely begun by my predecessor... This great commercial Metropolis ought to possess a Catholic Commercial College, worthy of itself and the Catholic name. We have excellent Classical Colleges in the Diocese and elsewhere, and they have proved by test to have reached a high state of proficiency; but we have no Commercial School, that I know of, coming up to the standard which I think we are bound to attain... We are a commercial people, and there is no reason why the Catholic Church should not supply as highly a Commercial education in Manchester as she does a liberal and classical elsewhere... We have peculiar advantages at our disposal in Manchester, and I desire to utilise them as soon as possible. I have already taken certain preliminary steps; but the time for public action has not yet arrived[1]".

It is significant that Vaughan had not been in Salford for a month when he announced his ambitious plans; there was insufficient time for him to have assessed and understood his new diocese and to have known if these plans would have worked in the area. Given the short time period, it is probable that both of these ideas had been conceived of at an earlier date and had been originally planned for the Diocese of Westminster.

The Seminary of Pastoral Theology

Vaughan immediately set about raising funds for his new seminary[2]. He held an open forum for the Clergy in the Cathedral Church Hall on the 14th May 1873, where he instructed them to begin fundraising efforts in their churches; he also approached local wealthy Catholic personages for donations.

The foundation stone of the seminary was laid on the 22nd September 1873, by Cardinal Manning[3], and the first students were admitted on the 28th October 1875[4]. The building alongside the Cathedral was expected to have cost around £7000, but

---

[1] VAUGHAN ACTA, vol. 1, p. 44-45, (Bishop Vaughan to Canon Kershaw, 30/11/1872).
[2] Ibid (Pastoral Letter on the Duty of Forming a Diocesan Seminary. 30/11/1872).
[3] Ibid, Pg161.
[4] LESLIE, S., 1948, *Letters of Cardinal Vaughan to Lady Herbert of Lea*, p. 271, 23/10/1875.

eventually spiralled to nearly £16,000. Canon John Beesley[1] was appointed as Rector; he was assisted by two full-time staff, Fr de Splenter and Fr Lawrence Johnson[2], while other clergy taught part-time. The first intake numbered twelve Divines being taught by four priests, but by 1887 there were only four Divines under two priests. The institution failed to provide a full-time education and often resulted in the Divines sitting around or being 'farmed' out to assist at local churches and it was never a success.

The seminary shut in 1892, when Canon Beesley resigned from the Cathedral due to ill health and Bishop Vaughan was elevated as Archbishop of Westminster. The project had been a failure and a costly one for the Diocese. The buildings were later adapted as administration offices for the Diocese and became known as Bishops House, then later as Cathedral House.

Planning for the Commercial College

The first mention Vaughan makes of his Commercial College idea after his initial 1872 announcement is in a letter to Lady Herbert of Lea in February 1874; "...I liked Lord Ripon[3] much. He entered into the idea of the Commercial College which I must plan, but defer working at till the Seminary is finished[4]". Other than this brief mention, the project has clearly been put onto a 'back-burner'; the diocese was expending large sums of money on the seminary and was in no position to afford a new High school.

In December of that same year at the annual Salford Diocesan Synod, Father Gallwey SJ[5] informed Bishop Vaughan of his "desire to establish a College in Manchester[6]". Vaughan reacted angrily to the news and expressed his disquiet immediately to Gallwey and refused to grant him permission. Within a couple of days he wrote to Lady Herbert, "I have a mess with the Jesuits, Father Gallwey being determined, to the ruin of the Xaverian Brothers' Middle School and the frustration of my intention to found a Commercial College, to start a school in Manchester[7]". The Diocese claimed that when Bishop Turner had given permission for the Order to return to the city[8] it was on the condition that "the Jesuits were in no circumstances to have a school other than a primary School for the education of the poor children of their

---

[1] Mgr Provost John Beesley (1834-1910, Ord. 1862). Cathedral Administrator & Seminary Rector 1874-1892. Died as Rector at Stretford in 1910.
[2] Fr Lawrence Johnson (1840-1897 – Ord 1866). Died at Osbaldeston.
[3] George Frederick Samuel Robinson, 1st Marquess of Ripon, Viceroy of India (1827-1909).
[4] LESLIE, S., 1948, *Letters of Cardinal Vaughan to Lady Herbert of Lea*, p. 242, 8/2/1874.
[5] Fr Peter Gallwey, Jesuit Provincial (1873-76)
[6] BROADLEY, J., 2010, *Bishop Vaughan & the Jesuits,* Appendix 2, (Vaughan to his Agent in Rome, 20/12/1874).
[7] LESLIE, S., 1948, *Letters of Cardinal Vaughan to Lady Herbert of Lea*, p. 264, 24/12/1874.
[8] The Jesuits had returned to Manchester in 1867 and established the Holy Name Mission on Oxford Road; the Foundation Stone of the Church was laid in 1869.

Parish...and not to detract from the educational work of the Xaverian Brothers[1]". Fr Weld would later deny that there were any such agreements made.

The matter was almost immediately elevated to Rome where it was put before Cardinal Franchi[2] and one of the bitterest disputes between the regular and secular clergy began. It is not my intention to dwell too much on the dispute as it has already been well chronicled by the Rev. Dr John Broadley in his book 'Bishop Vaughan and the Jesuits' but a basic knowledge of the timeline of events is required to understand the situation surrounding the opening of St Bede's.

In December 1874 Vaughan instructed the Diocesan agent[3] in Rome to let Propaganda know that he had already acquired "a most suitable piece of land... the site is one of the best in Manchester[4]". At the same time he made a similar statement to Lady Herbert, telling her that he "had already bought the land and got some money for it[5]". Roberts asks the question how the Bishop, who "had been continuously short of money... speaks of purchasing land and having money for the school he wished to open" and describes the sudden appearance of these resources for the school as "an unexplained phenomenon, but extremely timely for a Bishop hoping to make a case in Rome[6]". We also know now that Vaughan's statements about the land are entirely untrue; he would not buy the site in Alexandra Park until nearly two years later in 1876 and the house in Grosvenor Square was rented, while the chapel had been purchased by Canon Toole as a chapel-of-ease - Vaughan was clearly being economical with the truth both to Lady Herbert and to Rome.

The Ackers Street Jesuit College

At the beginning of 1875 and a couple of weeks after the Synod, Vaughan left England for a two-month tour of the United States in the company of Fr Gadd[7]. In his absence Fr Gallwey went ahead and opened the Jesuit College on Ackers Street in one of the Holy Name buildings, commencing with a total of seven pupils, and when the Bishop returned, he found it a fait accompli. He was furious and ordered Gallwey to close the new school immediately and threatened to suspend the Jesuits from Manchester[8]; Gallwey disputed Vaughan's authority to do this and sought support from Rome. In the meantime, Ackers Street closed early for Easter, but when support

---

[1] RAFFERTY, O.P., *The English Jesuit College Manchester 1875*, Recusant History, vol. 20.2, p. 292.

[2] Cardinal Alessandro Franchi (1819-1878) Prefect of the Congregation for Propagation of the Faith, known as 'Propaganda'.

[3] The 'Agent' was Dr Henry O'Callaghan (1827-1904), Rector of the English College, Rome (1867-1887).

[4] BROADLEY, J., 2010, *Bishop Vaughan & the Jesuits,* Appendix 2, (Vaughan to his Agent in Rome, 20/12/1874).

[5] LESLIE, S., 1948, *Letters of Cardinal Vaughan to Lady Herbert of Lea*, p. 264, 24/12/1874.

[6] ROBERTS, I.D., 1986, *Jesuit Collegiate Education in England 1794-1914*, Durham theses, Durham University.

[7] Mgr Charles Joseph Gadd VG (1838-1908, Ord 1861), Bishop's Secretary 1872. 3rd Vice-Rector at St Bede's 1885-1891, Vicar General 1891-1908. Went to St Chad's in 1891 as Rector, then in 1900 to All Saints, Barton where he died 1/7/1908 age 70.

[8] BROADLEY, J., 2010, *Bishop Vaughan & the Jesuits,* p. 44-45, (Vaughan to Fr Birch SJ, 16/3/1875).

came from Fr Beckx, the Jesuit Superior General, Fr Birch reopened it after the Easter holidays as planned[1]. However following further discussions in Rome, Beckx then sent new instructions to Gallwey that the school was to be shut again, and at the end of the Academic Year, the Ackers Street College closed for the final time.

The Chapel on Grosvenor Square

Canon Toole[2], Rector of St Wilfrid's, had since the 1860s run a Mass Centre at the St Alphonsus Infants School[3] and on the 7th July 1874, attained a re-mortgage on his church, in order to obtain £2600 needed to purchase a redundant Welsh Calvinist Chapel nearby in Grosvenor Square (next door to the Collegiate Institute) and thus relocate the St Alphonsus Mass Centre into a more suitable building[4]. The 1875 Catholic Directory records St Alphonsus Chapel as then being extant in Grosvenor Square. We know that the move angered the Jesuits at the Holy Name, and at the beginning of December, Gallwey wrote to Vaughan to complain. Sadly this letter has not survived but Vaughan's response was: "I quite enter into your feeling about the new chapel in Grosvenor Square. I should be sorry if it were to be an injury to the interests of the Holy Name. It is some yards – not a great many – nearer to your mission than St Alphonsus School, which has for years served as a chapel on Sundays, to the great inconvenience of the school and of the people. I do not imagine that it will be a permanent public chapel[5]". Vaughan's statement here that the chapel was not to be permanent is interesting as the Mass Centre was clearly required and Toole had taken out a large mortgage on his church in order to purchase it for just this purpose; we also know that this mortgage would be a burden on the Hulme mission as late as 1894 when it was finally transferred to the then independent Mission of the Holy Family[6].

---

[1] BROADLEY, J., 2010, *Bishop Vaughan & the Jesuits,* p.57, (Vaughan to Fr Birch SJ, 4/4/1875).
[2] Canon Lawrence Toole (1807-1892, Ord. 1841). Canon in 1852. Became Rector at Hulme in 1846 and remained there until his death.
[3] Catholic Directory of England & Wales, 1866, p. 114.
[4] Salford Diocese Deed Index, p. 331, Hulme, St Wilfrid.
[5] BROADLEY, J., 2010, *Bishop Vaughan & the Jesuits*, (Vaughan to Gallwey, 7/12/1874).
[6] SDA Finance Board Minute Book, Vol 3, p. 106-108, 31/10/1894.

The building in Grosvenor Square occupied by the Catholic Collegiate Institute 1864-1908.

This picture shows it in its incarnation as the Manchester Ear Hospital

The Welsh Calvinist Chapel in Grosvenor Square that became St Alphonsus Chapel then the Oratory of the Holy Family. The building visible on the right of the picture is the extension to the rear of the Collegiate Institute. The building on the left of the picture is the Chorlton Poor Law Union Offices.

The Crescent, Salford.
The buildings of the Salford Catholic Grammar School are in the middle of the picture; the site is today occupied by the Salford University, Research and Graduate College Building.

Mgr Augustus de Clerc
SCGS
1st President 1862-1889

Fr John Bromley Cooke
SCGS
2nd President 1889-1891
St Bede's College
4th Vice-Rector 1891-1894

Canon Peter Benoit
St Augustine's, Granby Row
Bishop's Secretary
2nd Rector of Mill Hill

The buildings of the Salford Seminary of Pastoral Theology
Salford Cathedral is on the left

Canon John Beesley
Rector of the Seminary
1874-1892

Part Two
The Rectorship of Fr Wood
1876 to 1877

Canon Charles Walter Wood
1st Rector 1876-1877

The Arrival of Fr Wood

Fr Charles Walter Wood arrived in Manchester from the Whitworth Mission in August 1875, one month after the closure of Ackers Street[1]. He took up residence at 16 Devonshire Street[2], Grosvenor Square – a substantial three-storey Georgian end-terraced house, which was leased from the Manchester Carriage & Tramways Company, who had their depot to the side and rear of the property. The house was described by Cardinal Manning as "temporary premises, until the intended new buildings shall be erected on the adjoining land which has been purchased for the purpose... the rooms are large and numerous; there is one lecture-room capable of seating 70 boys, allowing them all the space and area exacted by the standard regulations for Government schools. The room is well lighted and well ventilated and has several class-rooms in connection with it[3]". What was the land being referred to here? As far as we can ascertain there was never a site in Grosvenor Square purchased by the Diocese for St Bede's.

Fr Wood had been born on the 6th November 1838 into an Anglican family of prominent solicitors. He was received into the Catholic Church at the age of fourteen, allegedly by Canon Toole at St Wilfrid's, and at the age of sixteen he was sent by Bishop Turner to Ushaw to attend Junior Seminary. He was also possibly at the Salford Catholic Grammar School during the intervening years. At Ushaw, Wood proved himself an able scholar and the College archives tell us he was promoted early to the higher classes and remained top of the class listings, particularly in Latin[4].

In 1861, Turner sent him to continue his studies at The English College, Rome where he spent the next five years. Again he excelled and stood out amongst his fellow students; he was selected to represent the College singing in the Sistine Chapel and he was later invited to preach in Latin before the College of Cardinals and was honoured with a private audience with Pope Pius IX, to whom he then presented a copy of his discourse. He was ordained in 1866 in the Basilica of St John Lateran, after which he returned to Manchester where he was appointed to assist Canon Toole as junior curate at Hulme[5].

Hulme was by that point one of the most difficult missions in the Salford Diocese, heavily overcrowded and in the midst of one of the worst slums in Europe; the work was difficult and living conditions were harsh. Fr Wood laboured in the district for about four years until he suffered a serious breakdown of health which nearly proved fatal and he was forced to retire for a period from missionary duties. It seems likely

---

[1] Whitworth, St Anselm, parish registers record his final baptism on 22nd August and the first of his successor on 29th August.

[2] The property would later become The Victoria Dental Hospital and would be demolished in 1908 to make way for the Cavendish Board School.

[3] MANNING, Cardinal H.E., *Speech at the opening of St Bede's College*, p. 18, 9/1/1876.

[4] UCA, student records.

[5] Salford Diocese, Clergy Visitations, personal reports, 1874.

that Fr Wood never fully recovered either mentally or physically from this illness; from August 1870 he served a two-year period at the rural mission of St Mary, Blackburn, after which, in December 1872, Bishop Vaughan sent him to Whitworth to take charge of the church of St Anselm, a mission which was described as being "in a state of dilapidation and heavily burdened with debt and regarded as an almost a forlorn hope". It was reported that after a couple of years' work Fr Wood was once again "at the state of physical collapse", a fact which apparently when reported to Vaughan was met with the somewhat callous reply that "it was the glory and boast of the apostles and therefore of the secular clergy to suffer and die for the faith[1]".

So what was Wood doing in Grosvenor Square in August 1875? Manning claimed the following January that "for several months the Rector has been devoting his time and attention to the special study and examination of the modern working, methods and practices of some of the best public schools of the country[2]". His arrival did not go unnoticed by the Jesuits and Fr Greenan SJ wrote immediately to Gallwey to advise him of the development;

> ".... A Rev. Wood has been appointed to All Saints – formerly of St Wilfrid's, a convert, - I suspect he is to take charge of the chapel there and to be head of the school. I hear the brothers are up in arms – but I have no reliable information. I will set out this evening and put a friend or two 'on tracks'. The said Mr. Wood is a most zealous and, energetic little Priest, but when he was at St Wilfrid's he used to speak so vilely of the Jesuits that he disgusted even some of his best friends. I was told this by the 'friends' themselves...[3]"

The Jesuits here suggest that the Xaverians are unhappy about Vaughan's attempts to establish his college in Grosvenor Square, just as a few months earlier Vaughan had claimed the Jesuits were determined to ruin the Institute – both parties appear to be using the Congregation as a bargaining chip. The Catholic Directory of England & Wales for 1876 (printed late 1875) also raises some interesting questions:

> **1876 -** St Bede's Manchester College, 16 Grosvenor Square, Oxford Road, Fr Charles Wood, Mass; Sunday 10am. St Alphonsus, Grosvenor Square, Chorlton on Medlock (served from St Wilfrid's) – Mass; Sunday 10.15am

The first point of note is that St Bede's College is recorded as being in existence, months before it would open; there were no pupils, no staff and yet the Catholic Directory listed it. The second point is that the clergy from Hulme are still celebrating 10.15am Sunday Mass in the chapel, while a few yards away Fr Wood is celebrating 10am Sunday Mass in his house; if Fr Wood was still on 'active service' why had he

---

[1] THE HARVEST, vol. XIX, no. 220, Jan 1906, p. 5.
[2] MANNING, Cardinal H.E., *Speech at the opening of St Bede's College*, 9/1/1876, p. 18.
[3] BROADLEY, J., 2010, *Bishop Vaughan & the Jesuits*, p. 139 (Fr Thomas Greenan SJ (Holy Name) to Fr Gallwey SJ (Provincial), 25/8/1875).

not assumed responsibility for services at the chapel - particularly if the chapel was part of St Bede's College which was apparently open?

One possibility is that Wood was actually on sick-leave; the state of his health at Whitworth would certainly support this, and that he was living at the house in Grosvenor Square to recuperate and although it was not the healthiest place to convalesce, his presence there would certainly have been convenient for Vaughan, who was at the time having to justify to Propaganda the closure of the extant Jesuit school in favour of his, still theoretical, Commercial College, and with Wood resident in this large house, he could announce the building as being St Bede's and Wood as being the Headmaster.

Another interesting question is why Vaughan chose to dedicate the college to St Bede. His personal devotion was to St Joseph, and it was to him that he dedicated both the College at Mill Hill and the Rescue Sisters Congregation. There is a suggestion in the 1903 history that it had been the original intention to dedicate the Pastoral Seminary to St Bede. The origin of the College motto is also curious; the idea for commissioning a Coat of Arms was first mooted in January 1881 and was unveiled in December 1883. The motto 'Nunquam Otio Torpebat appears to owe its origins to a quote from a 17th century Benedictine Breviary, published on Mount Pannone in Austria, which said "Nunquam torpebat otio semper legit"[1].

Relations between Vaughan and the Jesuits deteriorated rapidly throughout 1875 and the Jesuits threatened to reopen Ackers Street in the New Year. Consequently in October Vaughan announced to Propaganda that "This school [St Bede's] will be opened on the 1 January and will as I have said be run by the Clergy of the Diocese[2]". This was the first time that the impending opening had been announced. Wood now had two months in which to get the house ready and Vaughan had two months in which to find his first intake of students. At the December 1875 Diocesan Synod, Vaughan announced to his clergy "the proximate opening of S. Bede's Manchester College, and solicited the interest and co-operation of the clergy in a work which he regarded as essential to the organisation of the Diocese[3]".

The Opening of the College

In January 1876, Cardinal Henry Manning arrived in Manchester with two duties to undertake; the opening of St Bede's, and the inauguration of the Academia of Catholic Religion. The ceremonies commenced on Sunday 9th, when he preached at the opening of the Oratory of the Holy Family, Grosvenor Square, giving a sermon on St Bede, his life, work and death, followed by a description of the new school[4]. It is not known why the decision was taken to rename the Chapel of St Alphonsus or why it was decided to

---

[1] Proprium Sanctorum, Vienna, 1693.
[2] BROADLEY, J., 2010, *Bishop Vaughan & the Jesuits*, p. 150, (Vaughan to Franchi, 28/10/1875).
[3] Salford Diocesan Synod, 21/12/1875, Point 14.
[4] St Bede's College Log Book, vol. 1, 1876-1881, p. 2.

reopen it, when it had already been open for public worship for nearly two years, except obviously that it provided maximum publicity for the new College.

On the following day, Manning gave a second speech; the inaugural address of the Manchester branch of the 'Academia of Catholic Religion', an intellectual society founded in late 1864 in London by Manning himself under the direction of Cardinal Wiseman. He described the primary purpose of the Academia as the "cultivation of the intellect and the advancement of science, making the Word of God the interpretation of His works the illustration of His word, and the science of God the centre and light of the manifold and various orders of human knowledge". There were lectures given and papers published. The chapel of St Alphonsus would serve for some years as the 'Hall of the Academia'. At the conclusion of his lecture Manning said he would like to "congratulate the Bishop of Salford that in the city of Manchester, in which, with a vigorous and fervent authority, he has already welded together the spiritual organisation of the church, he has successfully founded this intellectual agency, by which the young, perpetually rising from our schools, may receive such culture in literature and science that his flock be abreast, at least, with the highest cultivation of this great city[1]".

Following the inauguration, on Monday 10th January 1876, mid-way through the Academic Year and one week into the term, the first pupils were enrolled at St Bede's; they numbered just 14. Over the following months a further 21 would join, making a total of 35 boys. On Tuesday 11th Vaughan wrote to Lady Herbert to boast "We opened St Bede's College on Sunday and Monday and began with more than twice the Jesuits commenced with. Yesterday we inaugurated the Academia, which will unite the older and higher classes[2]". It is clear that Vaughan is still obsessed with one-upmanship over the Jesuits, particularly with regard to St Bede's.

Within a few days of the opening of the new College, Vaughan and Gadd once again left Manchester, this time on a three-month continental tour to Rome, via Belgium and Holland, later incorporating Spain and Portugal, and they would not return to the Diocese until mid-April. He told Lady Herbert that he was seeking European priests to join the Diocese[3]; the Manchester Examiner stated that his trip was to inspect the English Catholic Colleges on the Continent. However, his ultimate agenda would seem to have been to gain an audience with Propaganda in Rome, but by doing this he left his fledgling College with only Fr Wood to guide and establish it. An interesting participant in this continental tour was Fr Thomas Wrennall, who would become 2nd Rector of the College, eighteen months later.

The first advertisement for the new school made the following statement:

---

[1] MANNING, Cardinal H.E., *Inaugural Address at the Academia of Catholic Religion, Manchester*, 10/1/1876.
[2] LESLIE, S., 1948, *Letters of Cardinal Vaughan to Lady Herbert of Lea*, p. 276, 11/1/1876.
[3] Ibid

> "This College, which is under the general supervision of the Rector [Fr Wood], consists of two distinct departments – the High School and the Middle School. The former is under the immediate care of the Rector and the latter under that of the Xaverian Brothers[1]".

Cardinal Manning also stated at the opening; "The middle school now incorporated with the New College and hitherto known as the Catholic Institute... this school has now become a department or division of St Bede's Manchester College[2]". So the official impression given is that the Collegiate Institute was no longer an independent school and was at this point merely a department functioning under the overall control of Fr Wood, and this was after Vaughan had fought for the school's existence and independence, claiming that the Jesuits were trying to supplant it.

If we consider the attitude of the Xaverians the last time the Diocese had tried to interfere in the affairs of the Congregation in 1852 and the fact that they had invested so much time and money in the school when they finally gained control of it, it is unlikely that they would have taken this annexing of their authority lightly.

The First Academic Year

Wood was joined in January by four lay staff members; Dr Henry Cooke Foye BA PhD (Paris) taught 'Higher-Studies' and Mathematics, and also tutored for the Civil Service exams; Mr Thomas Flannery, late of St Mary's College, Hammersmith, taught English and drawing; Mr Charles O'Neill, the noted Manchester Analytical Chemist, taught chemistry at the school and Walter Howard St Ruth gave callisthenics classes. There were also two members of the clergy assisting; Fr Franz Schneiders[3] of Treves taught German and was Chaplain to the Oratory and Fr Octave Raymond[4] of the Brussels Conservatoire taught French and Music. When Vaughan returned from his trip to the Continent on the 10th April he decided to make immediate changes to the staff: he sent Fr James Moyes[5] as 1st Vice-Rector, teaching penmanship, book-keeping, drawing and civil engineering, as well as Fr John Vaughan[6] as Maths Professor, while removing Fr Raymond, Fr Schneider and Mr Flannery. Deacon William Fowler arrived in July as the 1st Prefect of Discipline[7].

---

[1] St Bede's College, Prospectus, January 1876.

[2] MANNING, Cardinal H.E., Speech at the opening of St Bede's College, 9/1/1876, p. 18.

[3] Fr Franz Schneiders (1848-1905, ord. 1873) was a German priest who came to England in 1875 as a refugee from Bismarck's Kulturkampf persecution, he is last recorded in the Diocesan annals in 1883 when he is assisting at Mount Carmel, Ordsall. Later that year he entered a Capuchin Order in Bavaria.

[4] Fr Octave Raymond was one of the young Priests brought to Salford from Belgium, by Vaughan. He went in 1887 as Rector to St Mary Magdalene, Burnley, retired in 1903 and died in 1910.

[5] Canon James Moyes taught at the Commercial College through its entire 18 year history. In 1892 when Vaughan was translated to Westminster; Moyes went with him as secretary. He became a Monsignor in 1897 and died in 1927.

[6] John Stephen Vaughan was the youngest brother of the Bishop; he was on the staff 1876-77 then returned to the College as Maths Professor 1879-1886. He became Auxiliary Bishop of Salford in 1909 and returned to St Bede's as 5th Rector 1912-1915. He died at Great Harwood in 1925.

[7] College Admission Register, vol. 1, 1876-1891, p. 4.

If we examine the student demographic of the first year's intake we find that three of the students had come from the Salford Catholic Grammar School, two were former pupils of the ill-fated Ackers Street Jesuit College with another two joining from the Jesuits at Stonyhurst, but the largest group were the eight students who moved from the Collegiate Institute, another fact which must have helped to exacerbate relations with the Xaverians.

There is also an unusual note with regard to the ages of the pupils who enrolled; eight of them were under the age of 11 with the youngest being only 7 years old. It is not clear why Vaughan was admitting elementary age school-children into St Bede's - the school was in no way equipped or staffed to provide for them. Of the remaining students, eighteen were in the 11-14 age group and eight were in the 14-16 age group[1]. The evidence therefore suggests that Vaughan was desperate to fill the school with anybody he could get, regardless of age.

On the 24th July 1876, the 1st Annual Prize Giving and Speech Day was held at the College. Vaughan was absent and sent Provost Croskell[2] VG to preside. Fr Wood gave the main address and reported on progress; he talked first about the students and staff who had joined and then went on to explain the lack of academic achievement during the first six months:

> "With regard to the progress of the students, I must premise that we have laboured under the ordinary disadvantages of every similar beginning. We have now only an existence of six months. During that time the students have come at intervals, breaking in upon the course. Some have been found to be extremely backward and neglected in point of instruction; and some, arriving from different schools, have had to be formed and trained to a new method. With all these disadvantages, however, much good and solid work has been done and I take this opportunity of stating that the laborious and painstaking efforts on the part of the Professors have been all that could be desired[3]".

Following this he praised and thanked the absent Bishop for his "kind and unceasing interest and constant support". Finally he made a statement on financial matters: "With regard to the finances of the College I may state that the means at my disposal have been administered with care and economy and that the accounts in connection with the College have been regularly and officially audited and found to be correct at the close of each preceding term[4]". Such a bold and clear statement must have been made for a reason!

---

[1] St Bede's College, Admission Register, vol. 1, 1876-1891.
[2] Mgr Provost Robert Croskell VG (1808-1902, ord. 1835). Rector at St Chad's (1842-1859), founded Stretford Mission in 1859, Rector at Levenshulme (1866-1903).
[3] St Bede's College, Log Book, vol. 1, p. 35 (First College Report by Fr Wood, 24/7/1876)
[4] Ibid

One of the most commonly repeated errors in St Bede's College history is that the Xaverian Collegiate Institute was entirely absorbed into St Bede's in the 1880s. The belief is understandable but quite inaccurate. While this had clearly been Vaughan's intention, the complete amalgamation never took place. When the College removed to Alexandra Park, the Manchester Examiner printed an article stating that the Collegiate Institute was moving as part of St Bede's, but Fr Wood corrected this in a subsequent letter to the editor that was published on the following day: "The contemplated removal to Alexandra Park referred to in your account today affects the department of the High School only. The old Catholic Institute, known now as the Middle School of the College under the management of the Brothers and numbering about 80 boys, remains, as heretofore in Grosvenor Square[1]". Casartelli would later state that "the union did not last long[2]".

The statement of the total amalgamation was first written up by Mr Whalley in his two-part history of St Bede's published in Baeda in 1926, when he echoed the statement made in his MPhil in 1923 and this was then referred to and repeated by Roberts in 1987. In fact the Collegiate Institute remained in Grosvenor Square and would in the 1880s be separated from St Bede's again. In 1908 it removed to Victoria Park and was afterwards and to this day known as Xaverian College.

The 2nd Academic Year

There were four new arrivals on the staff for the 2nd Academic Year: Fr Patrick Lynch[3] was appointed to teach Maths & Science, the post being made vacant by Fr John Vaughan's resignation due to ill health[4]. Fr Arnold Nohlmans[5] and Fr Franz Xavier Reichart took over the teaching of German, while Miss Mary Benaghan[6] was appointed as Governess to the Primary Department.

By July, Vaughan had decided to move St Bede's away from Grosvenor Square and was on the look-out for a new location. He wrote to Lady Herbert "I have had and have an unusual amount of anxiety in trying to find and buy the most eligible place in Manchester for St. Bede's College[7]". This is a contradiction to what he had said to her and to Propaganda eighteen months earlier when he had claimed to already have the site; even six months earlier he had expressed the intention to Lady Herbert that "I hope to be able to set up St Bedes's College on a good footing and to put up a good

---

[1] Diary of Mgr Gadd, 30/8/1876, (newspaper clipping).

[2] SDA157, Bishop Casartelli Letter Books, p. 76, Casartelli to Cox, 20/6/1910.

[3] Mgr Patrick Lynch (1852-1921, ord – 1876) Professor at St Bede's (1877-79), Rector at Hulme (1892-1914) and St Gregory, Farnworth (1914-1921). Canon in 1903, Provost in 1912, Mgr in 1915.

[4] Fr John Vaughan sailed to Australia on the 17th November 1876, to join his brother Archbishop Roger Vaughan in Sydney.

[5] Fr Arnold Nohlmans. Ordained 1876. Founded the Mission of St Saviour's, Burnley in 1892.

[6] Mary Beneghan, would become College Matron in 1877, she retired to Harrow on the Hill in 1900, where she died within a couple of years.

[7] Leslie, S., 1948, *Letters of Cardinal Vaughan to Lady Herbert of Lea*, p. 282, 12/7/1876.

building[1]", but did not make clear where it was he intended to build. It was mentioned by Wood at the July 1876 Speech Day that "the present premises are too small, and must be vacated before the first year has passed. Already steps have been taken to secure a position in a salubrious locality, with a view to the erection of suitable buildings[2]".

Monsignor Gadd recorded in his diary for the 18th July 1876: "Darbyshire's house bought from present tenant Mr Downes for £2500. It is situated in Alexandra Road about ½ way up Alexandra Park, best site in Manchester without exception". Alexandra Park was, in 1876, a gated community where the fashionable élite of Manchester lived in spacious landed detached villas. The new premises was a substantial double-fronted detached villa called Ebenezer House, and was located near the corner of Alexandra Road and Wellington Road. The building deeds record the official date of transfer as being the 18th August 1876; it was to serve as the residence of the Professors. Vaughan stated to Lady Herbert that "It is the finest site in Manchester. I shall have to build and am getting plans drawn by several architects who send them in on the chance of their own being chosen[3]". The plans were to extend on the vacant field to the North and rear of Ebenezer House with a commodious school block. The house was purchased by Vaughan's agent Mr Constantine Kelly, who bought the property for a 'Catholic bachelor friend' as it was feared that if the vendors knew it was being purchased by the Catholic Bishop of Salford, then bigotry could arise[4].

On the 3rd August, Mgr Gadd recorded in his diary that "Mr Hansom to call respecting S. Bede's, 10am – went to St Bede's, spent the day drawing out a plan, but Bishop gave him clearly to understand that he was by no means committed to accept it or even acknowledge it in any way[5]". We have no surviving record of what these original plans were, except for the fact that they would have been on the site today occupied by the Regis Building.

The 2nd Academic Year commenced on the 11th September 1876, with the teachers in residence at Alexandra Park but the classes still taking place at Devonshire Street[6]; the staff made the two-mile journey on foot.

On the 19th September, Cardinal Franchi (Propaganda) made a visit to Alexandra Park in the company of Cardinal Manning to see St Bede's College for himself. The students were marched from Grosvenor Square to Alexandra Road to meet him. Franchi's visit in itself was unusual: for the Cardinal for the Association of the Propagation of the Faith to come to England and to Manchester to visit a small

---

[1] Leslie, S., 1948, *Letters of Cardinal Vaughan to Lady Herbert of Lea*, p. 275, 31/12/1875.
[2] First College Report Given at the First Annual Distribution of Prizes, 24/7/1876, Fr Wood.
[3] Leslie, S., 1948, *Letters of Cardinal Vaughan to Lady Herbert of Lea*, p. 283, 28/8/1876.
[4] Snead-Cox, J., *The Life of Cardinal Vaughan*, vol. 1, p. 306.
[5] SDA, Diary of Mgr Gadd, 3/8/1876.
[6] College Log Book, vol. 1, p. 38, 11/9/1876.

provincial school was unprecedented. But the reason why he was brought to the Professors' residence in Alexandra Park rather than the rented school house in Grosvenor Square is likely to be connected to the fact that he had been told the site had been purchased four years earlier.

In March 1877, the villa on the South side of Ebenezer House, 'Rose Lawn', was also purchased by the Diocese, to serve as the school-house and on the 9th April, 16 Devonshire Street was vacated and returned to the landlord.

Fig 1 – The costs of the Alexandra Park property;

Property	Price	Mortgage
Ebenezer House	£2,750	£2,100
Rose Lawn	£1,410	£1,600
Aquarium	£6,950	
Hampton Grange	£1,250	£1,022
Total	**£12,360**	**£4,722**

The Manchester Aquarium

One of the primary reasons for Bishop Vaughan's decision to settle St Bede's on Alexandra Road was the presence of the Manchester Aquarium in the vicinity; this he understandably felt would provide a useful educational resource for the College.

In the 1860s advances in technology had enabled the creation of artificial deep-marine environments and it had become a fashion for inland aquariums to be established in towns and cities across the country. The idea for the Manchester Aquarium was first conceived of in 1871, when a group of local businessmen and marine-biologists met to discuss the proposal. The Manchester Aquarium Co Ltd was registered on the 12th April 1872 and the site measuring 120 square yards on Alexandra Road was purchased. A Manchester architect, Mr Joseph Sherwin[1], was engaged, and designed an elaborate complex in the Italianate style; the centre of the site was to be dominated by a great hall flanked by side corridors and would be surrounded by conservatories, aviaries, greenhouses and a winter garden.

As work began on site, the Board of Directors began to quarrel over the running of the new company and several members resigned in protest; the architect was sacked and replaced and then the new architect was also dismissed and he too was replaced. Plans had to be reduced and scaled down[2] and when the Aquarium opened on the 21st May 1874, only the great hall and flanking corridors had been completed, with a small suite of offices and a refreshment room at the rear. The Directors however were

[1] Joseph Sherwin (1837-1883). Emigrated to Oregon, USA in the late 1870s.
[2] MANCHESTER GUARDIAN, 14/9/1872

successful in engaging the services of one of the country's foremost marine biologists, Mr William Saville-Kent FLS FZS[1], as curator.

1876 was a bad year for the aquarium. The institution was failing to attract public interest and several attempts were made to entice more visitors, including the acquisition of a pair of alligators and the reduction of the entry fees from 6d to 5d, but despite these efforts the company continued to lose money. Saville-Kent resigned as Curator and the board continued to be caught up in petty squabbles, one example of which was over the question of whether alcohol should be available in the refreshment room[2]. At the AGM, the Board announced bad news: "To account for the previous heavy loss they explained the imperfect construction of the sea-water tanks in the first instance led not only to their reconstruction, but was the cause of great loss from the escape of water, which had been obtained at considerable expense... another item of similar loss had arisen from the great mortality of the fish during the two years[3]".

In July 1877, just over three months after the relocation of the St Bede's School-house to Rose Lawn, the Aquarium Chairman announced to the press that it was "a source of deep regret to the Directors that they had to recommend the winding up of the company". He attributed this "in consequence of the apathy that was shown on behalf of the public generally and the shareholders in particular". The shareholders voted in favour and the Manchester Aquarium Company was placed in administration[4]. Initial attempts were made to persuade the Manchester Corporation to purchase and run it as a public institution and on the 2nd August the Council Members met to discuss the proposal; it was unanimously rejected. The aquarium was then placed on the open market.

The Opening of the Boarding School

On the 9th April 1877, three of the students took up residence in Rose Lawn as the first boarders: the Log Book states that they were "the first Bedians[5]". Upon the completion of the Hampton Grange extension, the boarders took up temporary residence in the new servants' dormitory, until the students' dormitory in the South Wing of the College Building was completed.

There were two types of boarders accepted at the College in these early days. Parlour Boarders were the boys whose parents paid for private or semi-private rooms, and they were initially accommodated at Ebenezer House with the Professors, then later on the 2nd floor of the main building. The standard boarders were accommodated

---

[1] William Saville-Kent (1845-1908) was late of the British Museum and the Brighton Aquarium; his childhood had been marred by the murder of his half-brother and the conviction of his sister for the same. William was suspected of involvement but was never charged. The case was later catalogued in 'The Suspicions of Mr Whicher' by Kate Summerscale. He would eventually return to end his career at Brighton.

[2] MANCHESTER GUARDIAN, 15/7/1875.

[3] Ibid, 20/6/1876.

[4] Ibid, 5/7/1877.

[5] College Log Book, Vol 1, Pg 45

in three dormitories on the 3rd floor of the building; Fr Jackson later recalled these rooms in his memoirs;

> "Upstairs from here, if you go up and turn right, I think it's two rooms now, well that was one huge room, which was the Junior Dormitory, which was for the kids of ten and eleven. In my last year I was the big panjandrum in there: I had to sleep in that room and keep order, as well as I could. Next along, in the middle of the building, was the second dormitory, where I spent a lot of my life, and the third room at the very end was the senior dormitory and there I ended my days at St Bede's...The dormitories were a bit grim because there was no heating in them at all and we each had a wash bowl and jug which were left down the middle of the rooms which we had to fill up the night before. I remember that in the winter the water in the wash bowls would freeze, and you could take the whole thing out in a big block; I suppose that's why I'm so tough. The beds were curtained off in the Middle and Senior Dormitories but not in the Junior Dormitory, which was open-plan. There was one bathroom opposite the Matron's room, which had six baths in it. We were only allowed baths very occasionally on a rota, but we generally tried to avoid them[1]".

Of the overall 433 students who attended the Commercial College, 180 would board at the school (41%), the majority of these being the overseas students.

The St Bede's Mission, Alexandra Park

The Alexandra Park Mission of St Bede was erected by the Diocese on the 29th October 1876 and two rooms on the ground floor of Ebenezer House were converted into a chapel, shared between the school and the local congregation. On the 26th January 1877 the Aquarium refreshment room[2] was opened instead, Bishop Vaughan wrote on the occasion: "...On Monday I opened the new Chapel of St Bede in the back of the Aquarium. It was simply beautiful, thoroughly Roman...[3]" The Mission expanded fast and in September 1879 Sunday Mass was relocated to the Aquarium Main Hall.

Thoughts turned as early as 1880 to the idea of building a permanent church for the district and in November "a board [was] erected in the nuns' garden at the corner of Alexandra and Wellington Roads with the words 'Site of St Bede's Church (new church) [4]'". However Fr Hill admits in the Log Book that the sole purpose of this was to avoid payment for the paving of that part of Alexandra Road fronting the site; the

---

[1] Memoirs of Fr B. Jackson, 2004.

[2] This small room was located at the rear of the main hall; it later became the Billiard Room and was demolished in 1938. The site is now occupied by the Gonne Building.

[3] LESLIE, S., 1948, *Letters of Cardinal Vaughan to Lady Herbert of Lea*, p. 295, 01/1878.

[4] College Log Book, vol. 1, p. 123, 2/11/1880.

attempt was unsuccessful. Shortly afterwards on the 20th November 1880 Oswald Hill[1] sent in a design for a proposed church of St Bede, which he had prepared at the request of Vaughan – this was also never built and Hill notes in the Log Book that there was also never any intention of building it[2].

Fr Hayes as Vice-Rector was made responsible for the Alexandra Park Mission in September 1877; he was later succeeded by Fr James Rowan who in 1893 was assigned the responsibility of separating the Mission from the College. The new site further up Alexandra Road was approved by the Diocese in November 1893[3] and the church designed by FH Oldham[4] was opened on the 5th July 1896 by Cardinal Vaughan, who returned to Manchester for the ceremony. The name The English Martyrs first appears in the Diocesan Annals in April 1896.

The Clergy resident at the College also retained responsibility for the Holy Family Mission in Grosvenor Square, as well as the Chaplaincy to Withington Workhouse[5].

Fr Louis Charles Casartelli

While St Bede's was being established, the young Fr Casartelli (whom we last saw at the Grammar School) had been ordained at Salford Cathedral on the 18th August 1876 and then sent back to Louvain to further his studies for another year and to obtain his MA. On the 15th December, almost a year after the opening of St Bede's, Vaughan began a series of regular communications with him about the progress of the College. It was his intention that when Casartelli returned to Manchester he would take up a senior position there, and in 1877 Vaughan sent him on an investigative tour of Commercial Colleges across Europe[6].

He was first sent to the Institute at Antwerp where Vaughan asked him to investigate "methods made of encouragement, of punishment, of rewards and stimulus[7]". Six months later Casartelli was still touring and Vaughan asked him to "...note the letter of books, prices and publishers – when they seem to be any good. Also take note of the incitements and praises used to promote study, also enquire salaries of teachers[8]". What is interesting here is that Vaughan is seeking details of

[1] Oswald Hill was a Catholic Architect with his offices in Albert Square and an old boy of the SCGS; he was also a cousin of Mgr Gadd. He died in 3/1/1911 in Malta. His son Harry was a pupil at St Bede's (1897-1903). He later took over his father's practice, but was killed in WW1. The practice was then taken over by Henry Sandy (1868-1922) who went into partnership with Ernest Bower-Norris (1888-1969) and the firm was known as Hill, Sandy & Norris. In the 1930s Bower-Norris took Hill's nephew Frank Reynolds into the practice, along with William Scott; they took over the partnership in 1947 and renamed it Reynolds & Scott and in the 1950s they were responsible for designing the Beck Building.

[2] College Log Book, vol. 1, p. 124, 20/11/1880.

[3] Salford Diocese Finance Board, Minute Book, vol. 2, p. 64, 29/11/1893.

[4] Francis Haslam Oldham (1844-1908), President of the Manchester Society of Architects 1900-01.

[5] Salford Diocesan Almanac, 1883, p. 36.

[6] SDA179

[7] SDA179, Vaughan to Casartelli, 15/12/1876.

[8] Ibid, 6/1877.

fundamental basics of running the school – and yet the school had already been operational for upwards of eighteen months!

The First Crisis and the Sacking of Fr Wood

The situation at St Bede's didn't improve during the 2nd Academic year and on the 4th May 1877, Vaughan wrote to Casartelli: "...We have no plans of St Bede's yet, only the work of drawings are being made. I am looking forward to your coming home to relieve me from a world of anxiety and troubles. I have deemed Fr Wood to keep on in Status Quo and to let the changes to take place when you have got into the work and can organise a system of instruction[1]". The College was failing to achieve any level of academic status and Vaughan put his hopes on Casartelli being able to deal with the problems.

However, less than four months later when Casartelli did arrive in Alexandra Park, he found that Wood had left the previous day. The College Log Book records the official line that Wood "retired from the Rectorship". Yet a couple of days later in a letter to Lady Herbert, Vaughan stated that "St Bede's has been going through a crisis. Father Wood has made way for a more efficient Rector[2]". The tone of this letter suggests that Wood has been sacked, and by the term 'efficient' Vaughan clearly means 'competent', but was Vaughan being fair putting the entire blame on the Rector? Certainly St Bede's had failed to establish itself during these initial eighteen months, but was it actually his fault?

The possibility certainly exists that Wood's level of competence in the role as Rector may have stunted the development of the school and if we examine his later career we do see some recurring themes. After leaving the College in 1877, he went as Rector to St Mary, Swinton, where he remained until 1892 when he was appointed to Ss Peter & Paul, Bolton. He retired from the Diocese in March 1901 to live at Llandudno, where he died in November 1903 at the age of 65. His successor at Swinton, Fr Andrew O'Rourke, wrote the following damning critique in 1900:

> "[I] Took possession of Mission in February 1892. I have had to take up the work here of a dishonest cur – he made a mess of the place and then was allowed to clear off and leave his mess behind him… [he] has been allowed by the late Bishop to take away with him when leaving here, the mission account book of this mission; this act of theft has been confirmed by your Lordship… [My main problems are] the legacy of bungling and trickery which I have inherited from my predecessor[3]".

[1] SDA179, Vaughan to Casartelli, 4/5/1877.
[2] LESLIE, S., 1948, *Letters of Cardinal Vaughan to Lady Herbert of Lea*, p. 290, 18/8/1877.
[3] Salford Diocese, Mission Inspection Returns, 1900.

We also see if we examine the parish registers from Swinton that Wood takes a very inactive role. The registers are in some disarray and Wood performed less than a quarter of the total number of baptisms during his tenure, seemingly leaving his curates to undertake the day-to-day work[1]. This was unusual for the day and was only generally seen if the priest was elderly or infirm, but curiously, despite these failures at St Bede's and at Swinton, in 1892 we see Wood appointed to the Cathedral Chapter and given a larger and more important mission by Vaughan.

So either through frail health or general apathy, Wood was certainly not the most 'efficient' of priests, but was it surprising that the school failed to thrive? It had been opened prematurely mid-way through the first Academic Year, filled with children as young as seven, despite being a High School; the buildings were undoubtedly inadequate in Grosvenor Square and the later semi-move to Alexandra Park separated the staff residence from the classrooms. Vaughan, the man who had conceived the idea and who was essentially the only man who knew exactly what the school was to be, had left the country for most of the first Academic Year and Wood had an untrained and untested staff with no experience of this new commercial and experimental education system, while the bitter disputes between St Bede's and the Jesuits and the Xaverians must have also created an unsavoury atmosphere in Chorlton on Medlock.

So the possibility certainly exists that Wood was put into a 'no-win situation' by his Bishop in 1876 and then used as a scapegoat when things went wrong and the questions still remain: considering his frail health, should he ever have been put into the situation at all? and similarly should the College have been opened in January 1876, in such a clearly unprepared state? If the answer to these questions is 'no' then at least some of the blame should surely be directed towards the Bishop himself.

[1] Parish Registers St Mary, Swinton, SDA CD.

The pupils and staff of St Bede's during the 1876/77 Academic Year, pictured on the steps of Ebenezer House.

The original 1876/77 St Bede’s College Staff, pictured in front of Ebenezer House: Fr Francis Reichart, Fr James Moyes, Fr Charles Wood, Fr Patrick Lynch & Deacon William Fowler.

The original architect's design for the Manchester Aquarium—only the central hall and flanking corridors were ever built and today form the Academic Hall, Lady Corridor and Library Corridor.
At the top left of the picture can be seen Hampton Grange (the College Lodge).

Mgr James Moyes
1st Vice-Rector 1876-1877
Professor 1877-1892

The Cenacle Convent was established in Ebenezer House (above) in 1880; the above picture is circa 1900 with the convent buildings wrapped around the original house.

The Retreat House (below) was opened in 1910 on the adjoining plot.

Part Three
The Rectorship of Mgr Wrennall
1877 to 1891

Monsignor Thomas Wrennall
2nd Rector 1877-1891
1st Procurator 1891-1894
In residence 1894-1903

"Father Wood has made way for a more efficient Rector and a staff of Ushaw Professors[1]"

The Staff of Ushaw Professors

On the 6th September 1877, the Rev. Fr Thomas Wrennall took up residence at Ebenezer House as the 2nd Rector of St Bede's College. Casartelli had already arrived the previous month in the position of 1st Prefect of Studies, as had Fr James Hayes[2] on the 3rd September as 2nd Vice-Rector. The newly ordained Fr William Hill[3] moved in on the 9th September as the 2nd Prefect of Discipline. The former Vice-Rector, Fr Moyes (although reduced to the ranks), remained on the staff along with Fathers Patrick Lynch, Franz Reichart and Octave Raymond, and lay-masters Charles O'Neill, Francis Simpson and Walter St Ruth[4].

Born in the Fylde in 1828, Wrennall was the third of four brothers, all of whom entered the Priesthood; the eldest brother Mgr William Wrennall DD served as the 9th Rector of Ushaw (1878-1885); the second brother Fr Joseph Wrennall was 13th Prefect of Studies there (1859-1869)[5], while the youngest Canon Henry Wrennall laboured in the Diocese of Hexham. Thomas Wrennall was also at Ushaw, going there in 1841 and remaining for fourteen years, including a period in the post of Minor Classics Professor prior to his ordination in 1854[6]. In the Diocese he served an eight-year period as Rector of St Mary, Oldham, ending in 1869 when due to a breakdown in health he retired and took the post of Chaplain to the Good Shepherd Convent at Blackley; at this time he was also appointed as Chief Inspector of Schools for the Diocese. He was nearly 50 when he arrived at St Bede's and was elevated to the Cathedral Chapter on the 18th April 1878, then became Monsignor on the 21st July 1880, when Vaughan, during his two-year stay in Rome, petitioned Pope Leo XIII to appoint him a Cameriere Segreto[7]. This would set a precedent, whereby nearly all future Rectors of St Bede's College would also be elevated to a similar position. We can examine the character of Mgr Wrennall through a series of memoirs collected for the Diamond Jubilee of the College in 1937:

---

[1] LESLIE, S., 1948, *Letters of Bishop Vaughan to Lady Herbert of Lea*, p. 290, 18/8/1877.

[2] Canon James Hayes (1837-1900 – Ord. 1861) Rector at Swinton 1867-77. 2nd Vice-Rector at St Bede's 1877-86. Canon in 1882. Ill-health forced his retirement, but he spent his convalescence at St Bede's until was appointed Rector at All Saints, Barton in 1890 and died there in 1900.

[3] Fr Hill had been Minor Professor at Ushaw; he remained on the staff at St Bede's until 1891 when he lost his job as part of the College reorganisation made necessary by the merger with the Grammar School. 2nd Prefect of Discipline (1877-78). He also served as Bishop's Secretary (1877-1891) and Diocesan Chancellor (1877-1901). He was appointed Monsignor in 1906 and died at Samlesbury in 1929.

[4] College Log Book, vol. 1, p. 118, 10/9/1877.

[5] MILBURN, D., 1964, *A History of Ushaw College*, p. 286-292.

[6] THE HARVEST, vol. XVII, no.198, March 1904, p. 60-61.

[7] College Log Book, vol. 1, 21/7/1880, p. 109.

"Mgr Wrennall had all the qualities that were characteristic of the old type of Lancashire priest. His piety was simple, unaffected, and unashamed. He was shrewd yet frank, parsimonious yet generous, stubborn yet gentle. In other words, there was always going on inside him a struggle between the man in the office and the father in God. Ideals ruled his life and conduct, yet he was always merciful, or better, sympathetic towards those who fell short of his ideals… quite unconsciously Mgr Wrennall made a profession of integrity and the natural virtues. There was nothing subtle in his composition. He registered plainly his feelings and emotions, which he never let beyond control. A boy guilty of anything 'ungentlemanly' in conduct might not in his presence feel guilty of actual sin, but he certainly felt very much of a criminal[1]." (Anon, Baeda 1937)

"[Mgr Wrennall] A fine man, full of tact, sound judgment, and common sense. No nonsense if you know what I mean. He was the right type for dealing with men and boys.[2]" (Mr M.A. Sullivan – staff: 1879-1926)

The Rector was a very genial, elderly (to us) priest, and he was beloved by all of us because he was always fair and kind to us, even when we really deserved punishment, but we did not abuse it. I remember one occasion when Fr John Vaughan was in charge of a 'Penance Class' in one of the classrooms – the partitions of which did not reach the ceiling - and some of us decided to raid the class with snowballs. Next day all the students were assembled in the 'Hall' and the Rector explained the seriousness of the affair and put us on our honour for all involved to come before him. The appeal was so strong that we all sheepishly walked up to him[3]". (Henry F. O'Brien – OB: 1879-83)

Essentially Wrennall, with his teaching experience at Ushaw and his role as Schools Inspector, was probably the best qualified member of the Diocesan Clergy to take on the St Bede's project, although it should be noted that his experience was still only in Classics and not in Commerce.

St Bede's & the Aquarium

Vaughan was immensely disappointed when it was announced that the Manchester Aquarium was to close and thus deprive his students of its educational services. However, as soon as the announcement was made that the company was in administration, he wrote to Lady Herbert: "... the aquarium is to be sold by auction August 1st, but it has a ground rent of £270 a year which is fatal[4]". His initial thought was that if he purchased the building, it could be converted into a church to serve the new Alexandra Park mission and he attempted to repeat the ruse used to buy Ebenezer

---

[1] BAEDA, new vol. 12.1, Easter 1937, p. 38-39.
[2] Ibid, p. 45.
[3] Ibid, p. 6-9.
[4] LESLIE, S., 1948, *Letters of Cardinal Vaughan to Lady Herbert of Lea*, p. 289, 7/1877.

House, with Constantine Kelly acting as "agent for a Catholic bachelor friend"; however this time news was leaked of the plans and the local residents reacted angrily, writing to Lord Egerton in protest; "This week we have learnt that the Manchester Aquarium, which was built on a portion of your Lordship's estate is to come onto the market and that the Roman Catholic authorities have made an offer for the building... we feel compelled to say that we cannot contemplate the acquisition of the building for Roman Catholic Church with other than feelings of anxiety.[1]"

With such strong objections, Vaughan initially withdrew his interest in buying the building. However when the only other party to show its hand was the owner of a local entertainment company who felt that the great hall would make an ideal 'Music Hall', the local populace found the idea even more abhorrent than the concept of it becoming a Catholic Church and Vaughan, who was also incensed at the prospect, decided that he had no choice but to look once again at purchasing it; negotiations began and the contracts were signed on the 29th August 1877:

> "I have bought the Aquarium!! And all its fishes, crocodiles and alligators, the building and the land for £6950. The buildings, tanks, etc., cost over £21,000 and had the main building to be erected at present prices, it would cost one-third more than the original price. I was finally compelled to buy by the probability of its going into the hands of a man who would have converted it into a music hall and tea-gardens. This would have ruined St Bede's... It is not to be for a church. The people of the Parish must build their own, though we may use it temporarily as such: but for a Museum, Exhibition Hall.[2]"

Vaughan was very aware that in buying and closing the aquarium, he could find himself accused and blamed for depriving the city of its cultural heritage and that he could be labelled as something akin to a Visigoth. It is interesting that the line taken by the Manchester Guardian on the acquisition was simply a dry comment about a "Napoleonic Stroke" and a suggestion that "Bishop Vaughan and his clergy may now enjoy a large fish and chip supper[3]". Vaughan subsequently decided that he would allow the aquarium to remain open, but only on the condition that it was used: "I have given a Board leave to see whether it is still needed by the Manchester people as an Aquarium. I shall be desperately pushed for a time, I dare say, to meet the liabilities, etc., but have no fear but that Providence will pull us through[4]". However, his inexperience at marine and aquatic management was soon all too evident as one famous anecdote tells us:

> "On one occasion a conger-eel was expected, as well as specimens of several varieties of sea trout. To economise carriage from the coast the trout were taken out of the tanks in which they were being conveyed and put in with the conger-

[1] St Bedes College, Log Book, vol. 1, p. 56, 31/8/1877, (Letter, Alexandra Park Residents to Lord Egerton).
[2] LESLIE, S., 1948, *Letters of Cardinal Vaughan to Lady Herbert of Lea*, p. 291, 2/9/1877.
[3] MANCHESTER GUARDIAN, 3/9/1877.
[4] LESLIE, S., 1948, *Letters of Cardinal Vaughan to Lady Herbert of Lea*, p. 291, 2/9/1877.

eel. When the professors at St. Bede's came to examine the consignment on its arrival, a lethargic conger-eel was found to be the solitary occupant of the tank.[1]"

After just over two months, it became clear that the people of "Manchester declined to be interested in what the advertisement described as 'the lessons taught by the finny monsters of the deep'. The aquarium wore a melancholy air. There was something depressing in that silent solitude of fish and reptiles" and on the 7th December the Aquarium Management Committee recommended to Bishop Vaughan that he close the institution immediately to prevent further financial losses for the diocese as "the receipts are inadequate to meet the current expenditure". He immediately began preparations to enact the recommendation. The School Log Book records that the "27th December 1877 was the last day on which the aquarium was open to the Public, a concert in the large hall at 8pm for the benefit of the curator and other servants employed in the aquarium. The snow lay over a foot deep on the ground and helped to make the concert a perfect failure[2]". The live exhibits were sold to the Yarmouth Aquarium and to Mr G.H. King of London[3]. The Bishop wrote to keep Lady Herbert updated: "...We are getting the fish out of the Aquarium and are going to turn it into classrooms for the present...[4]"

The Log Book records for the 31st December 1877 "As many of the fish etc from the tanks as could, began to be sent off and during the next few days all the tanks were cleared of water. A circular had been issued by the Board of Management inviting tenders for the fish, fittings etc, etc" and it was then that the Bishop and Fr Wrennall had their unfortunate and now famous encounter with the resident alligator which needed moving for transport, as recorded by Snead-Cox:

> "...The Bishop, who, owing to his wanderings in South America, was generally understood to be an authority on alligators, was appealed to. He explained that all that was wanted was a coffin-shaped box, open at one end; this should be put against the door of the reptile's cage; then it would only remain to tickle the creature's tail with a twig to make it move. These instructions were faithfully carried out; unfortunately, however, the door of the cage was found to be wider than the end of the box. To remedy this defect a piece of wire netting was held on either side of the cage door to make a passage to the mouth of the box. For some moments the alligator seemed to pay no attention to the twig that was tickling his tail then suddenly catching a glimpse of one of the fingers holding the wire netting in position, it made a rush, and with such vigour that the fingers let go, the netting fell, and the reptile was free. The blocks of masonry which had been used to support the fish tanks fortunately provided convenient islands of refuge from which the would-be captors [Bishop Vaughan & Fr

---

[1] SNEAD-COX, J., 1910, *The Life of Cardinal Vaughan*, vol. 1, p. 313.
[2] St Bede's College, Log Book, vol. 1, p. 187, 27/12/1877.
[3] Ibid.
[4] LESLIE, S., 1948, *Letters of Cardinal Vaughan to Lady Herbert of Lea*, p. 293, 12/1877.

> Wrennall] were able to look down, in safety, upon the alligator as he wandered at leisure around the hall[1]".

College lore tells us that the hapless alligator had to be shot and was later stuffed and displayed in the school museum. On the 9th January, the final meeting was held of the Aquarium Board of Management. The remaining parts of the aquarium were dismantled gradually; the Log Book records that on the 10th June 1878 "The tanks in the North and South aisles of the late aquarium began to be taken down. Most of the glass and other objects sold to the Manager of the Edinburgh Aquarium" and finally over the Summer Holidays 1879 "The tidal and shallow tanks which ran the full length of the interior of the Hall on the North and South Walls removed".

College Buildings

With the purchase of the aquarium, Vaughan was once more forced to change his plans for St Bede's College. The school would now no longer be built around Ebenezer House and Rose Lawn on the south side of Wellington Road; instead the plot on the north side of Wellington Road would be the base. On the 5th January 1878, classes were held in the aquarium buildings for the first time as recalled by Mr Henry O'Brien in 1937; "The old aquarium was being transformed into a College by temporary makeshifts of classrooms in the two corridors by the side of the Academic Hall… the partitions of which did not reach the ceiling[2]".

On the 17th November 1877, Hampton Grange, the villa between the Aquarium Hall and Wellington Road, was purchased from the Barker family[3] and was renamed St Bede's Lodge. In the following year extensions were built to the rear of this house, providing a refectory and kitchens on the ground floor, with a dormitory above for the domestic staff; the extension was commenced on the 13th October 1878 and it was occupied on the 12th September 1879[4].

> "The long winter made a serious delay in our building operations. It is cheering to notice the rapid progress which has been made since the spring began to show itself. The new refectory will be ready for use very soon after Easter. This handsome room, 48ft by 27ft, will accommodate over 100 persons. A handsome Dado of pitch pine is being made in Scotland, to run round the walls. To the west side are the Kitchens and offices. The large dormitory over the refectory will be temporarily appropriated to the students[5]".

---

[1] SNEAD-COX, J., 1910, *The Life of Cardinal Vaughan*, vol. 1, p. 312-313.
[2] BAEDA, new vol. 12.1, Easter 1937, p. 7 (memories of HE O'Brien).
[3] A notable local Catholic family; two of the Barker sons, Ernest & William, were pupils at St Bede's. William was killed in a road accident in 1898. Ernest was one of the pupils who attended the Rhine House in 1886. He fought in WW1 and saw action at Gallipoli, he emigrated to Australia after the war. Their mother Mary is commemorated on a plaque in the College chapel.
[4] St Bede's College, Log Book, vol. 1, p. 83, 18/10/1878.
[5] St Bede's Magazine, no. 1, April 1879, p. 16.

The main College Building was designed by Edward Joseph Hansom[1] of Dunn & Hansom and was described as being a Florentine Palazzo in the Italian Renaissance style; the completed building was to be over 300ft in length and consist of a four-storey rectangular block of ten bays, arranged on either side of a central vestibule covering the front of the former Aquarium and flanked at the North and South Ends by five-storey towers of two bays. The building was constructed of orange brick with terracotta facings (as these were cheaper than stone). The Manchester Guardian described the plan as "classic design, very similar to the new buildings erected in the extension of Stonyhurst College[2]". The reference to Stonyhurst is interesting; was Vaughan still trying to compete with the Jesuits, in the design of the building? One thing is certain - it was massively in excess of the requirements of the College at the time.

It was decided to build the new structure in three stages with Mr William Healey[3] as contractor, the 'first brick' of the South Wing was laid on the 18th February 1878, with the Foundation Stones being laid on the 16th May by the Duke of Norfolk, Lady Annette de Trafford, and Messrs Murphy and O'Neill. At the end of March 1880, the ground-floor classrooms were used for the first time (despite building work continuing on the upper floors) and on the 20th May 1880, with all the Staff and pupils entirely resident in the newly completed wing, Ebenezer House and Rose Lawn were vacated by the College[4] and then turned over to the Sisters of Perpetual Adoration from Belgium.

Funding for the new building was obtained through an idea of Bishop Vaughan's to approach the Catholic aristocracy and business community with the offer that they could become 'College Founders'; this meant that they would donate a suitably large sum of money (over £1000) to the building fund and in return their coat of arms would be displayed on the panelling in the College Refectory and their souls would be prayed for at the College, in perpetuity. Through this method Vaughan was able to collect ten thousand pounds: Manchester brewing magnate Mr Lawrence O'Neill gave £6000, while Sir Humphrey de Trafford Bart., Henry Fitzalan-Howard the 15th Duke of Norfolk, Mr Daniel Murphy of San Francisco and Abbot Hunter-Blair each gave £1000. Annual 'Founders' Masses' were held at the College well into the twentieth century, but have now been discontinued (see appendix 5).

The South Wing, when finished, provided: on the ground floor, three large classrooms with a study-hall in the tower, on the first floor, the Rectors apartment and

---

[1] The Hansom family were a dynasty of Catholic architects; Edward was nephew of Joseph Aloysius Hansom of Hansom Cab fame. The family were also the favoured architects of the Jesuits in England and had built the Holy Name Church, Manchester and extensions to Stonyhurst College.

[2] MANCHESTER GUARDIAN, 19/9/1879.

[3] William Healey (1821-1887) was a local Catholic building contractor, born in Ireland; he immigrated to Salford in the 1840s. In the 1881 Census he is recorded as employing 440 and was responsible for all the early College buildings. After his death, his son William Joseph continued the firm.

[4] St Bede's College, Log Book, vol. 1, p. 103, 20/5/1880.

a series of meeting rooms, with a library in the tower, on the second floor, living quarters for the staff and rooms for Parlour Boarders, and on the third floor two large dormitories, while the rooms in the top of the tower provided a sanatorium with an isolation area. The initial South Wing cost just under £13,000 to complete[1].

An additional building was added to the campus at the latter end of 1882, being occupied in January 1883. This was located at the west end of the Academic Hall and comprised a two-storey classroom block which would mainly be used for science laboratories: "Went with Bishop to see new classrooms at W. End of building. Selected centre one for museum. Appropriated others for various classes[2]". Despite these additions, more space was soon needed, and as early as July 1882, Vaughan announced "I am also going to put up the centre block of St Bede's College. The inconvenience at present is very great. It will cost, I fear, £5000 or £6000[3]". The Foundation Stone was laid on the 18th July 1883 by Humphrey Francis de Trafford[4], and it was officially opened on the 4th September 1884.

It was then decided to put the final part of the building on hold until such a time as the number of pupil's resident at the school warranted its construction. However, the Commercial College never reached this stage and it would only be after the 1891 merger with the SCGS that the requirement for the completion of the building would be first discussed. Fundraising recommenced in 1906 and in the early 1920s, Bishop Casartelli reignited the project and even went so far as to lay the foundation stone on the 23rd July 1924[5]. However following Casartelli's death in January 1925, the new Bishop, Thomas Henshaw[6] put a halt on the project in order to undertake a full review. By 1928 the estimated costs had gone up to £80,000 and Henshaw stated that the "idea of finishing the College in the present style is now impossible and from an education point of view, foolish[7]" and the project was officially terminated. In 1934, the Rector Mgr Gonne described the main College building as "A fine building... but one quite undesirable as a school and quite inadequate in accommodation[8]".

---

[1] St Bede's Magazine, no. 18, Jan 1881, p.123.
[2] SDA F161, Bishop Casartelli's Diary, 17/1/1883.
[3] LESLIE, S., 1948, *Letters of Cardinal Vaughan to Lady Herbert of Lea*, p. 348, 6/7/1882.
[4] Humphrey Francis de Trafford (1862-1929). Eldest son of the College Founders, he succeeded to the de Trafford titles upon the death of his father in 1886 and within 15 years had bankrupted the family and forced the sale of Trafford Hall & Park, to pay his debts.
[5] BAEDA, new series vol. 8.4, Jan 1925, p. 2.
[6] Bishop Dr Thomas Henshaw (1873-1938 – Ord. 1899). Old boy of the SCGS. Joined staff at St Bede's and was 7th Vice-Rector (1905-1912), elected 5th Bishop of Salford in 1925.
[7] SDA 210-112.
[8] BAEDA, new series vol. 9.1, March 1934, Pg2.

The Lay Staff

Although during the 1880s St Bede's was mainly staffed by members of the clergy, there was also a core of laity employed, some who lived on site and others who travelled in. Among the most notable lay professors were: Mr Michael Sullivan, Head of Mathematics (1879-1926); Mr Edward Pyke, Head of Modern Languages (1885-1926); Mr John J. Cardwell, Head of Geography (1884-1922) and Mr Fridolin Landolt who taught French (1880-1897). One item worthy of note from Figure 2 is the disparity between the wages of the lay staff, about £25 a year, and those of the clergy, around £110 per year.

With such a large number of boarders and resident staff, a team of domestic servants was required to run the operation. The post of 'Matron and Housekeeper' involved managing this staff and the first person to fill this position was Miss Mary Ronchetti[1]. She resigned after only a year and was replaced by the primary school mistress, Miss Mary Beneghan who undertook the role from 1877 until September 1900. The 1881 census records Beneghan with a team of eleven domestics: cook, laundress, waitress and eight maids. By the 1891 census the team had increased to fourteen and included: porter, cook, valet, two laundresses and nine maids. The cost of running such a large domestic team was one of the financial burdens strangling St Bede's. In 1878, the servants' wages amounted to £240 per annum.

College Finances

Surviving in the College archives are some early annual income and expenditure statements for the school and what they demonstrate is that from the time of first opening, St Bede's was running at a massive deficit. If for example we examine the 1878 Accounts (Fig 2) we see annual expenditure of £3,594, with income of only £1,037, meaning an annual deficit of £2,557; in modern day values this would be approximately £117,000[2]. This was repeated in subsequent years and demonstrates how unsustainable the College was as a business. The only way to improve matters would have been to drastically increase the numbers of students attending the College and thus raise the income, but Vaughan was unable to do this and instead began borrowing large sums of money from Mill Hill College and from the Diocese in order to financially support St Bede's. By 1879, the former had loaned a total of £3,100 and the trustees of Mill Hill contacted the Diocese asking for guarantees that the money would be repaid[3]; later ownership of the College Cricket Field and the Rhine House would have to be signed over as security.

Presumably the Bishop believed that the College would grow at such a rate in the early years that there would soon be enough fee paying students to balance the books

---

[1] Mary Ronchetti was a sister of Louis Casartelli's mother. He lived at her house on the Crescent during his years at the SCGS; she left St Bede's over her treatment by certain members of the staff.

[2] http://www.nationalarchives.gov.uk/currency

[3] Salford Diocese, Finance Board, Minute Book, vol. 1, p. 58-83.

and repay the debts; this growth however never happened and the College ran at a loss for its entire sixteen-year history.

This led in 1894 to an acrimonious dispute between the College and Fr Hill, then in his capacity as the Diocesan Chancellor. Since Vaughan's departure from Salford in 1892, control of the College finances had passed to Mgr Wrennall as the new Procurator (Bursar). Hill was at the same time trying to control the Diocesan Finances in the wake of the Bishop's exit and the two clashed over accounting irregularities.

The Financial dispute related to:

1. The mortgage of £1600 on Rose Lawn which was still being paid by the College, despite the house having been sold to the Cenacle Sisters almost fifteen years earlier.

    Vaughan had taken the purchase money paid by the Sisters for the house and rather than clearing the outstanding mortgage had invested the sum in a plot of land in Horwich, along with £1000 loaned from the Rescue Society.
2. The £75 ground rent being paid by the Cenacle Sisters.

    As the College retained the freehold of this land, the ground-rent should have been paid to them. However, this sum was being used to maintain the annuity fund (see point 4)
3. A loan of £400 paid to St Bede's College from Diocesan Funds.
4. A sum of £1500 taken by Vaughan from Diocesan funds towards expenses connected with St Bede's College.

    This money was removed from a £6000 annuity fund being administered by the Diocese on behalf of a Miss Snape. As the sum of money was never repaid; the Diocese had to supply an annual interest payment of £80 to maintain the annuity, most of which came from the Ground Rent of Rose Lawn, money which was supposed to being paid to the College.

These financial arguments would continue at St Bede's until the 1920s.

Fig 2 – College Accounts 1878

	Expenditure	**Income**
Wages - Fr Wrennall	£300.00	
Wages - Fr James Hayes	£120.00	
Wages - Fr James Moyes	£110.00	
Wages - Fr Louis Casartelli	£110.00	
Wages - Fr Patrick Lynch	£110.00	
Wages - Fr William Hill	£110.00	
Wages - Fr Charles Browne	£110.00	
Wages - Fr Henry Formby	£110.00	
Wages - Mr Charles O'Neill	£25.00	
Wages - Mr Walter St. Ruth	£25.00	
Wages - Mr Gallus Oesch	£20.00	
Wages - Miss M.A. Benaghan	£110.00	
Wages - Fr T. Croskell (Part-Time)	£25.00	
Ground Rent & Rates	£1,366.00	
Housekeeping Expenses	£678.00	
Servants' Wages	£240.00	
Annual Stipends	£250.00	
Repairs & Maintenance	£75.00	
School fees and pensions		£952.00
Chapel Bench Rents and collections		£85.00
Total Expenditure	**£3,594.00**	**£1,037.00**
1878 Deficit	**-£2,557.00**	

The Sisters of the Cenacle

The Sisters of Perpetual Adoration arrived at Alexandra Park on the 6th August 1880; four nuns originally from Belgium moved into Ebenezer House, where they established the Cenacle Convent and the building was renamed St Gertrude's House. The house was officially purchased by the Sisters on the 1st May 1888, with six Belgian ladies signing the deeds, Sisters Laure Marie Mathilde, Valdruche de Montrémy, Pierette Françoise, Antoinette Dutel, Ida Emélie Guislane Richler and Marie Klien. On the 5th June 1895, a second conveyance exists between the Diocese and the Nuns; this is possibly when they also took over Rose Lawn[1]. They later purchased 'Avon Lodge[2]', the third and final house in the block, which had hitherto remained in the private ownership of Mr John Guerin.

Later in 1895 Oswald Hill was engaged to design a new convent which would incorporate the existing buildings. This was opened in July 1896 by Bishop Bilsborrow[3] and included a large chapel, entrance foyer, cloisters, living accommodation and a bell tower. By 1901 there were twenty-five Sisters in the community and by 1911 they numbered forty[4].

A decade later the convent would require further space and on the 27th May 1910 Bishop Casartelli opened a new building on the corner of Wellington Road; the four-storey redbrick block was designed to accommodate one-hundred women or girls on retreat[5]. Interestingly this was the site on which Vaughan had planned to build the College in 1876. Casartelli recorded in his diary in March 1912 "134 girls in retreat at Cenacle – largest number yet[6]", so the retreat facilities at the convent were clearly in great demand, very early on.

In January 1973 with the Convent in decline, most of the site was sold back to St Bede's and St Gertrude's House was demolished. The Regis Retreat House however was retained by the College[7], and between 1984 and 1985 it was converted into a new classroom block, which was opened in September 1985, to accommodate the growing numbers at St Bede's, which had become co-educational in September 1984[8].

The Pupils

The College Admission Register records the details of 435 students who attended the St Bede's Commercial School over its sixteen academic years; this is an average of 27 per year. What is apparent on examination of the register is that a large percentage of the pupils are foreign or primary school age boys, which is in conflict with Vaughan's original purpose in establishing St Bede's, which was to provide a commercial education for the high-school age sons of Manchester's Middle Classes.

In fact more than a third of the children who passed through the College were not English; 61 (14%) came from South America, with 34 (8%) coming from Europe and 34 (8%) from Ireland and Scotland. The first international student, Miguel Yuarazaval, arrived in September 1876 from Chile, and by April 1878 Vaughan had decided to

[1] SDA AP10, St Bede's Legal papers (unsorted).
[2] This is the only one of the three houses still standing; it survived the 1973 demolition of the convent and remained as the residence of the Sisters until the mid 1990s, when it was sold and converted to flats.
[3] THE TABLET, 25/7/1896, p. 27.
[4] Census of England & Wales.
[5] Ibid, 10/12/1910, p. 23.
[6] SDA F162, Bishop Casartelli Diaries, 9/3/1912.
[7] BAEDA, vol. 13.12, p. 517, spring 1973.
[8] Ibid, vol. 17.3, Autum 1985.

officially market the College across South America and had his youngest brother translate the prospectus:

> "Fr Kenelm Vaughan translated a Prospectus of the College into Spanish at the request of his brother Bishop Herbert Vaughan and issued a small Spanish pamphlet in connection with the College. They are intended for Extensive circulation in South America[1]".

With regard to the underage pupils, in 1877 St Bede's was forced to open a primary department at the College in order to accommodate them. Miss Beneghan was initially placed in charge as Governess; however in September 1882 Mother Mary de Sales of the Loreto Convent, Hulme was sent to take over and remained in the position until her death in July 1900[2].

The Admission Register also tells us that of the overall students, 178 left the College either at the end of, or during, their first year; this is 40%[3]. What all this demonstrates is that Vaughan was struggling to fill the places at St Bede's with the intended demographic, or to keep the students who were enrolling, and thus he was forced to look further afield to underage children and to foreign children, in order to keep numbers up.

If we examine the individuals themselves then the list of notable alumni is relatively lengthy for the small numbers; of the international students, four stand out, Narciso Lacayo (82-84) who became the Nicaraguan Consul in London, José Gutierrez-Guerra (83-86) who became President of Bolivia in 1917, Victor Eastman-Cox (85-86) who was appointed Plenipotentiary of Chile and Alavro M. de Brito (86-89) who became head of the Civil Service in Mozambique.

Fourteen would see military action. Richard Seed (78-82), Hubert Wolsley (88), Proper Paris (88-90) & George Dalton Leake (91) all fought in the 2nd Boer War: Wolsley was killed in action at Elandslaagte, both Seed and Paris were at Ladysmith, during the famous siege on that town, and Seed was 'Mentioned in Dispatches' for 'Conspicuous Gallantry'. In the Great War, Captain Leake would serve once again, but would die at Ypres in May 1915; his younger brother Major Claude Lancelot Leake (91-93) also served; he won the MC in 1918, the OBE in 1919 and the Médaille d'Honneur in 1920. Also on the Western Front were Lt William Connery (90); Captain William Henry Higginson (78-84); Captain Alfred Gadd (81-83), Ernest Barker (1881-88), who was at Gallipoli and Lt Colonel Geoffrey Hillers Swindells (86). Other conflicts involving old Bedians included the Sino-Japanese war where Dr Edward Thomas Meagher RN (87-89) served as Spanish interpreter and the Argentinian-

---

[1] St Bede's College, Log Book, 28/4/1878, p. 41.

[2] Following her death, a stained-glass window was erected in the St Joseph Chapel in her memory.

[3] There is also a number of the 435, for whom there is no leaving date recorded, so the percentage may be higher.

Chilean threat where Carlos, Daniel and Julio Leake were all conscripted into the Chilean army.

Ten of the students were ordained for the Priesthood: Mgr Provost James Rowntree (76-81), Canon Henry Chipp (76-80) and Fr Henry Hunt (77-79) for the Salford Diocese, Fr Charles Annacker SJ and Fr Daniel O'Neill SJ, as Jesuits, Fr Frank Matthew Middlehurst OSFC (86-89) as a Franciscan, Fr Terence Corrigan (77-79) for Portsmouth; Fr Robert Rooney (88-90) for Menevia, Fr Nathaniel Eastman (86) for Santiago, Chile and Fr James Mahoney (76-79) for Galveston, USA.

Other Bedians who made their name included: John O'Kane Murty (86) who became District Judge for Ratnapura, Sri Lanka; Dr John Farrington (76-81) who became President of Rotuma Island, Fiji; William Patrick Byrne (76-79) who became a senior central government civil servant and in 1922 was appointed Governor of the Seychelles, and John Joseph Meagher (76-84) who became head of Williams Deacon's Bank and who in 1920 was granted 'The Freedom of the City of London'.

Qualifications at the College initially consisted of an internal award called 'The Diploma of Association by Examination'; only five students attained this Diploma. In 1879 it was awarded to Terence Corrigan, James Mahoney and Bernard Benedict Hughes (78-79), in 1880 it was awarded to James Rowntree and in 1886 to Carlos Gomez (84-86). The school later registered with the London University & College of Preceptors Examination Board and through this, the annual exams were taken. In October 1896, the Oxford Local Examination Board was adopted instead[1].

[1] St Bede's College Log Book, new series vol. 2, 1895-1898, p. 54.

Fig. 3 - Numbers of new admissions to the Commercial College.

School Year	New Admissions	Day Boys	Boarders
1876	35	35	0
1876/77	18	14	4
1877/78	25	16	9
1878/79	35	17	18
1879/80	20	8	12
1880/81	20	6	14
1881/82	28	10	18
1882/83	36	7	29
1883/84	31	6	25
1884/85	31	11	20
1885/86	32	6	26
1886/87	37	14	23
1887/88	27	5	22
1888/89	20	4	16
1889/90	24	12	15
1890/91	14	9	5
	433	**180**	**256**

The Second Crisis

In January 1880, Vaughan left Salford for Rome and would not return until the following year on the 5th July 1881[1]. During this eighteen-month absence from his Diocese, St Bede's was left entirely in the hands of Wrennall and Casartelli, although the Bishop was not averse to trying to continue pulling the strings from afar, mainly through the medium of letters. As previously mentioned, he had arranged for Wrennall to be made a Monsignor, which was announced at the College's 5th Annual Speech Day on the 21st July 1880, but less than a month later another letter arrived for the Rector from Rome;

> "... I do not know what the result of the examinations has been, but from several quarters I have heard that the Speech Day was most deplorable. I do not know what the failure may be attributed to; I would only say for your general direction that I should consider it cheap to incur any expenditure and to make any sacrifice of money and men, rather that the College should obtain and

[1] McCORMACK, A., 1966, *Cardinal Vaughan*, p. 164.

> derive a bad reputation for teaching and learning. You can apply this principle according to your discretion[1]".

Vaughan here instructs Wrennall to spend whatever is needed to make St Bede's work. Later in the letter he makes a series of suggestions for changing the teaching methods, which he asks the Rector to pass on to Casartelli:

> "One thing I remember, used very much to be liked by Professors and Boys at one College where I was... at the beginning of the scholastic year, the Prefect of Studies used to inform each class publicly how much work (of each subject or another), how many written exercises, how many lines by heart, would have to be got through by each class, during the year. It was always a good full measure of work and used to be written up - and the Professors and Boys had it always before them during the year. It would have to be well thought out by the Prefect of Studies. I think such a plan if adopted by Fr Casartelli would give a more definite aim and would concentrate attention of each class upon the years' work and would keep the Professors and boys up to the collar[2]".

The following year at the 1881 Speech Day Casartelli announced in his Annual Report that "during the past year some effort, however small, had been made towards setting on afoot a system of higher commercial education such as was carried to perfection in foreign countries...[3]". The school was now in its sixth year and it was publicly stated that only small progress had been made. On the 25th September, Cardinal Manning made a surprise visit to Alexandra Park to inspect the struggling College[4]. In August 1881, a month after returning to England, Vaughan vacated Bishop's House, Salford, and removed his episcopal residence into the St Bede's Lodge (Hampton Grange). He then appointed himself 'College Director'. As usual he wrote to advise Lady Herbert of the developments:

> "...I have taken the College, St Bede's, very much under my own management and direction without replacing Mgr Wrennall, the ecclesiastical scarecrow whose face you will remember. He is very glad I have determined to take up the work. Otherwise it would fail".

St Bede's was once more at crisis point and Vaughan was clearly blaming Wrennall, in the same way as he had blamed Wood five years earlier. The reference here to 'the ecclesiastical scarecrow' is a somewhat cruel jibe at Wrennall's distinctively haggard and gaunt appearance. There is no record of the attitude taken, either by the Rector or by Casartelli, of Vaughan's coup-d'état, but it is clear that Wrennall has now fallen out of favour.

---

[1] SDA179, Vaughan to Wrennall, 18/8/1880.
[2] Ibid
[3] MANCHESTER GUARDIAN, 21/7/1881.
[4] St Bede's College, Log Book, 25/9/1880, p. 120.

> "Dr Herbert Vaughan lived in the house... and very often he would walk about the corridors that were available and take any student who might appear lonely or disconnected for a walk and have a friendly and stimulating chat with him[1]". (HF O'Brien)

College Sports & Extra-Curricular Activities

The first Annual College Sports Day was held at Trafford Park in May 1879, as guests of the de Trafford family, and in June of that year a 'Lawn Tennis Club' was established, with a court being built in the gardens behind the Academic Hall. Shortly afterwards a field was rented on Manley Road which was laid out as a cricket pitch and in February 1885, a new field was purchased on College Road, in two plots for a total sum of £4583[2], and a small pavilion was opened on the site in June of that year. The following memoir was written in 1937:

> "Such cricket as there was in the first two or three summers was played on the spare ground behind 'Rose Lawn' on what is now the site of the Cenacle Convent. It was apparently not until 1880 that a cricket ground was acquired. This was a field three minutes [away], bounded by Alexandra, Manley, Albert and Brantingham Roads, a ground which had been borrowed two summers previously for the first Athletic Sports (the second sports were at Trafford Park). This ground, a mere stone's throw from our present field, was in use for four years and here was played in 1880 the first Past and Present match, a victory for the Present. Here too was played an extraordinary game on September 27 of the following term, Cardinal Manning a frequent visitor to the College in Bishop Vaughan's time, asked for a game to be played in his presence, on a holiday granted in his honour. It is to be feared that Manning, who had captained Harrow against Eton at Lords over fifty years before, was disappointed with the game. The pitch was not good, the players out of practice, and they knew that His Eminence had been a slow bowler and a stylish batsman and was likely to be critical. At any rate, they were so ashamed of their performance that for the season of 81 everything was reorganised. Mr Sullivan took charge, and that was the real beginning of St Bede's cricket[3]". (GJS)

On the 8th December 1891, Vaughan transferred the cricket field from the Diocesan Trustees to himself and the trustees of Mill Hill College; he transferred the deeds entirely to Mill Hill on the 24th November 1893. This was, as previously mentioned, in repayment of some of the outstanding debts owed by St Bede's to Mill Hill.

[1] BAEDA, new vol. 12.1, Easter 1937, p. 6-9.
[2] SDA, Deeds of St Bede's Cricket Field.
[3] Ibid, Pg50.

In 1883, Vaughan conceived the idea of building an indoor playground for the College. Mr Healey was employed to build the walls, the Bishop having drawn up the plans himself, feeling that there was no requirement for an architect. He then commissioned Andrew Handyside and Co to build an iron and glass roof for the new playground; however when the framework arrived, Healey objected on the basis that the walls were insufficiently strong to hold up the roof and only agreed to finish the building if the Bishop signed a disclaimer absolving him and his company from any blame, should the building collapse. Eventually a compromise was reached whereby large buttresses were erected at either end of the hall to strengthen the walls[1]. The building for most of its history would be known as The Covered Playground; in 1980 it was refurbished as a gymnasium and renamed the Sports Hall[2].

Other extra-curricular activities included the Debating & Elocution Society, which was formed by Casartelli in November 1877. This society would survive ninety-six years until Summer 1973[3] and its activities were recorded in Baeda under the title of "8pm in the Library".

> "Mgr Wrennall was a great patron of the Debating Society. At 8pm in the library he was nearly always there. He had a bête noir: the absurd standard of voting for recitations. He would complain bitterly of reciters who had achieved only moderate success being voted nine and perhaps ten points by some of the boys. "Ten means perfection" he would say "and no one is perfect. Take nine for your maximum. If a reciter does well, give him six or seven. If he doesn't reach a high standard, give him four or three[4]". (Fr Charles Wilkin 1937)

Casartelli also formed a 'Meteorological Society' and his father Mr Joseph Casartelli donated a series of instruments to the College for the recording of the weather. From the 1st January 1878 the Society made daily observations (max and min temp and rainfall) and these were posted on the main door of the College[5]. By the end of the year, the Manchester Guardian and the Manchester Courier had taken a great interest in the affairs of the Society and asked for daily meteorological reports that could be printed in their newspapers – these were the beginnings of full records of Manchester's weather and would continue to be taken from St Bede's until February 1881 when testing was transferred to the Royal Botanical Gardens, Old Trafford[6].

It was also Fr Casartelli who first conceived the idea of establishing a Commercial Museum at St Bede's and suggested the idea to Vaughan in a letter in July 1877, in which he expressed his view on "the importance and prestige of museums[7]". The

---

[1] SBCA, Mgr Hill to Bp Casartelli, 31/8/1908.
[2] BAEDA, vol. 17.2, p. 12, autumn 1984.
[3] Ibid, vol. XIV, no. 1, June 1974, p. 23.
[4] Ibid, new vol. 12.1, Easter, 1937, p. 17.
[5] St Bede's College, Log Book, vol. 1, 1/1/1878, p. 48.
[6] Ibid, 22/2/1881, p. 137.
[7] SDA 179, Vaughan to Casartelli, 12/7/1877.

College inherited some exhibits and display cases from the Aquarium and in September 1878, the Log Book records that "Museum started. Curator; Rev. Fr Casartelli. An attempt at starting a museum had been during the Christmas Vacation (1877-78) when the tanks in the North Corridor were utilized for a few weeks as 'cases' but it proved to be merely a temporary display of a few specimens of odds and sods[1]". The following month, Vaughan travelled to the Colonial Exhibition in Paris to collect exhibits. Over the subsequent twelve years, the museum expanded greatly, but following the 1891 merger would gradually fall into disuse. In 1890 it was described as "a commercial and colonial museum of which no school in England possesses the equivalent[2]".

In 1928, Mr Whalley catalogued the contents for a series of articles published in Baeda when he described the museum as "only a shadow of its former self, our Commercial Museum in the chapel corridor still lingers on, almost unknown – a relic of bygone days[3]". Six years later Fr Charles Anselm Bolton[4] began the dismantling of the exhibits and by the beginning of the 1934/35 Academic Year, the display cases and their contents were gone[5].

The first attempt to launch a College Magazine was in October 1878, when the weekly St Bede's Gazette appeared for the first time; single copies were produced which were read out in the Refectory and only one issue is known to have survived[6]. After seven months 'The Gazette' was abandoned and replaced with the monthly St Bede's Magazine, which itself lasted for only twenty-four issues before it too was abandoned in July 1881, mainly due to the fact that the School could not afford to continue producing it. The institution of the College Magazine would not recommence until after the merger, when at Michaelmas 1896, Baeda appeared for the first time, but it too had to be abandoned after five years when recurring financial worries stopped production in 1901; it was recommenced in June 1910 and has been continuously produced since then. The Salford Catholic Grammar School also produced a journal, named Frondes Silvulae, the first issue of which was published in June 1879.

The College Associations

In the mid-1880s Vaughan decided that one way in which to make the Diocesan Colleges more financially independent was to encourage wealthy and successful alumni to become socially and thus financially involved in their alma mater. Initially this was done through 'Past and Present Matches', then later through Associations; the

---

[1] St Bede's College, Log Book, vol. 1, 10/9/1878.
[2] LeClerc, Max, L'education et la société en Angleterre, 1894.
[3] BAEDA, new vol. 11.2, May 1928, p. 5.
[4] Fr Charles Anselm Bolton MA BLitt, (1905-1970 – ord. 1930) served on the College staff 1930-1951 when he was appointed PP at Clayton-le-Moors; he wrote the history of the Salford Diocese in 1950.
[5] BAEDA, new vol. 9.3, Oct 1934, p. 85-86.
[6] St Bede's College, Log Book, vol. 1, 1/10/1879.

first mention of the proposed St Bede's College Association is in Casartelli's diary for 1885 when he mentions that on the 28th February, Mr JJ Kelly[1] visited him to discuss the plans. The Association was formed in March 1885 with the Rector as President, Ernest Annacker as Chairman, Charles Farrington as Vice-Chairman, Joseph Casartelli as Treasurer and John Kelly as Secretary. There were in total twenty members[2]:

> "The primary object of the Association is to form a centre of union for the Past Students and the Friends of St Bede's in whatever part of the world they reside, and to keep up by various means the connection between them and the College[3]".

A similar organisation was formed at the Salford Catholic Grammar School, meeting for the first time on the 29th December 1886 at the Grammar School. About eighty alumni were in attendance and a committee of twelve was elected. At the following meeting on the 19th January 1887, Fr Wood was elected as 1st Secretary[4] and was instructed to draw up the rules for the new Association, but he resigned within a week and was replaced by the architect Mr Oswald Hill. The 1st official General Meeting was held on the 8th March. By September the Association had organised itself to fund two new scholarships for two years to the Grammar School. Thirty-five members attended the 1st Annual Meeting in January 1888, when it was recorded that there were 5 Life Members, 2 Honorary Members and 46 Ordinary Members[5].

The two societies were merged together in 1893 and the St Bede's College & Salford Catholic Grammar School Association was formed with Oswald Hill as 1st Secretary.

St Bede's on the Rhine

> "In the summer of 1886, the Rt. Rev. Herbert Vaughan DD, Bishop of Salford passed several weeks in Germany in company with the Rt Rev. Mgr Canon Kershaw and during their tour they were very much struck by the Germans whom they found speaking English and French naturally and their conversation often turned upon the superiority of German students over English students in respect of foreign language and with the inadequate means placed within the reach of English boys who wished to acquire a good knowledge of foreign languages, without being obliged to submit to the un-English manners and customs of a foreign college[6]".

---

[1] Mr John Joseph Kelly (OB 1876-80, 1881-82)
[2] SDA F161, Bishop Casartelli Diaries, 28/3/1885.
[3] SBCA, Annual of the Association, 1891.
[4] There is no known record of Fr Wood actually being an old boy of the SCGS.
[5] SBCA, Salford Catholic Grammar School Association Minute Book.
[6] St Bede's on the Rhine, Log Book, p. 1.

Vaughan returned to England with another of his 'brain-waves': that branches of St Bede's College should be opened in Germany, France and Spain. He informed Mgr Wrennall of his plans and then announced them to the College staff and pupils on the first day of the 1886/87 Academic Year. On the 6th October, Monsignors Wrennall & Gadd were sent to Germany to find appropriate accommodation and to make the necessary arrangements for the first group of students. They returned to Manchester on the 25th of that month, having arranged for the party to be accommodated at the Hotel Weller, Oberlahnstein[1].

On the 17th November 1886, Mgr Wrennall led the first group of seven Bedians to Germany. In his absence, Mgr Charles Gadd was appointed Pro-Rector of St Bede's, Manchester. The party arrived at the Hotel Weller on the 20th and began organising the new College. Classes had been planned to commence on the 24th November but upon arrival at the school room they found the entire village shut down for a local holiday and the opening had to be put off to the following day[2].

On the 8th July 1887 Vaughan returned to Germany and wrote to Lady Herbert to report that the "ten boys from St Bede's have made only a moderate progress in German during the seven months they have been here[3]". His main reason for the visit was to find and acquire a permanent 'Rhine House' and by the 19th he reported that he was "in treaty for a palace in Bonn which formerly belonged to Prince Metternich and is one of the best houses there[4]". It is recorded in the Diocesan Annals that the Bishop borrowed another £3500 from Diocesan funds to purchase this house[5]. It was now that Vaughan decided to change the plans and intentions for St Bede's on the Rhine; the new idea was "to open a House for twelve or twenty German boys of good Catholic families and for ten or twelve English, giving the Germans the majority of the house; so as to make the German language the language of the college[6]".

In preparation for the new term in Germany, Wrennall went back to Germany in September assisted by the newly ordained Fr James Rowan as school-master[7], and the following month, the 2nd Academic Year of St Bede's on the Rhine commenced at Metternich, Bonn with four students from Manchester. Within a month, however, the German Government forced the closure of the school: Bismarck's anti-church regulations had placed restrictions on the power and authority of the Catholic Church and had insisted that any school had to be run by a Government approved Rector; Vaughan had also failed to seek permission to open St Bede's on the Rhine and in doing so was operating the College illegally. Leaving England on the 30th October, Vaughan rushed to Bonn to try and salvage the situation and was successful in

[1] St Bede's on the Rhine, Log Book, p. 3.
[2] St Bede's on the Rhine, Log Book. p. 12.
[3] LESLIE, S., 1948, *Letters of Cardinal Vaughan to Lady Herbert of Lea*, p. 384, 8/7/1887.
[4] Ibid, Pg 385, 19/7/1887
[5] Salford Diocese, Finance Board Ledger, vol. 1, Folio 270, 13/9/1887
[6] LESLIE, S., 1948, *Letters of Cardinal Vaughan to Lady Herbert of Lea*, p. 384, 8/7/1887.
[7] MANCHESTER GUARDIAN, 19/2/1935.

engaging the services of the Rev. Fr Loben, who had the necessary qualifications to be a Government approved headmaster and was consequently able to persuade Bismarck to permit the school to reopen[1]. Wrennall came home and resumed his position as Rector in Manchester at Easter 1888, leaving Rowan as the English representative in Bonn, assisted from 1890 by Fr Henry Chipp. A description of the school was published in the Guardian in 1891:

> "On the first floor were the school room, the chapel, and the professors' rooms: on the second and third floors, the boys dormitory – a large and pleasant room, with each bed curtained off and plenty of space for them all. Then leaving the building, we visited the outhouses and inspected the carpentering and fret-working rooms... both German and English students are admitted and all are boarders. Boys over fourteen years of age generally attend classes held inside the college. Those under that age attend the day classes of a large public school in the town[2]".

St Bede's on the Rhine was never a success. During its ten-year history only 27 pupils from Manchester availed themselves of its services, Vaughan's estimated plan of ten to twelve English students per year was never achieved[3] and the proposed sister houses in France and Spain were soon forgotten. Loben asked to be relieved of his post of Rector at the end of the 1892/93 academic year, wishing instead to go out on to the Mission[4] and he was replaced for the remaining years by Fr Christopher Joseph Bundgens[5], who remained in charge until the college closed[6].

In 1892, when Vaughan was translated to Westminster, he tried to persuade the students of St Edmund's College Ware to share St Bede's on the Rhine and the College Prospectus for 1893/94 stated that "Students who are going through their entire course at St. Bede's College, Manchester, or at St. Edmund's College, Ware, will have the advantage of the German House without any augmentation of the ordinary pension[7]". However the archives at Ware show no record of any students ever taking up the offer.

> "The chief reason why the scheme did not eventually succeed was the apathy of English parents, who did not realise sufficiently the very great educational advantage offered by this German branch of S. Bede's[8]".

---

[1] LESLIE, S., 1948, *Letters of Cardinal Vaughan to Lady Herbert of Lea*, p. 389, 13/11/1887.
[2] MANCHESTER GUARDIAN, 15/6/1891.
[3] St Bede's College, Admission Registers, vol. 1, 1876-1891.
[4] SDA 210-064, Rev J. Felton to Cardinal Vaughan, 25/12/1892.
[5] Rev. Bundgens became curate at St Remigius Church, Bonn, retired in 1916 with failing health and died in 1922.
[6] BAEDA, new series vol. 5.6, January 1922, p. 204.
[7] St Bede's College Log Book, new series vol. 1, 1891-95, p. 145-147.
[8] SALFORD DIOCESAN ALMANAC, 1903, Pg 49-50.

The financial battle which developed in the 1890s between Vaughan, the Diocese and St Bede's brought into question the ownership of the Rhine House and during the 1895/96 Academic Year, the experiment was abandoned and the property disposed of. A college myth later developed that the school had survived until 1914 and had been forced to close by the outbreak of the Great War, but this is entirely refuted by all available and known evidence.

When the College Magazine of St Edmund's Ware published an obituary to the Cardinal in July 1903, within the section detailing his career, they coyly asked of the Rhine house, "Whether, however, it produced an adequate return for the amount of labour and money expended on it, may be questioned[1]". This was a rare contemporary suggestion that Vaughan's illustrious career may not have been the overriding success that was being publicised by most at the time.

Deteriorating Relations

As mentioned in Part 2, Bishop Vaughan had determined that Fr Casartelli's future lay in running and developing St Bede's, even before the latter's ordination in 1876. However, Broadley suggests that "the post of Prefect of Studies was uncongenial to him, and far below his capabilities[2]". What is clear is that as the College failed to establish itself, Casartelli became disillusioned and Vaughan became impatient. Casartelli's attitude was evident as early as 1879, when he recorded in his diary: "To me the life of a Professor has been to some degree bitter and is continually full of anxieties, troubles, disappointments. What I would not give for the exchange[3]".

In January 1883, Casartelli's diary entries show more of his frustrations: "school began after Xmas holidays. We are short-handed: Fr Vaughan away ill at Abergavenny, Fr Moyes slowly recovering from measles – I take M's place". He went on to describe Moyes as a hypochondriac[4]. Evidence of further friction between him and Vaughan exists in letters from August that year; Vaughan had written to Casartelli to inform him that the Diocese was "to open a Grammar or Middle School at Blackburn" and suggested that two of the lay teachers be removed from the St Bede's staff to run it[5]. Casartelli clearly reacted angrily to the proposal, presumably on the basis that he was struggling to keep the College afloat and had worked hard to assemble his teaching staff. Although his reply has not survived, Vaughan's subsequent response was "...Respecting Mr Russell and Mr Morgan – I wrote for your opinion, intending to meet your wish. You have expressed it – with extra strength[6]". The following year, following the conclusion of the 1883/84 academic year, Vaughan wrote a long letter to Casartelli criticising his performance as Prefect of Studies:

---

[1] THE EDMUNDIAN, new series vol. V.31, July 1903, p. 164.
[2] BROADLEY, M.J., 2006, *Bishop Louis Casartelli*, p. 26.
[3] SDA F161, Casartelli Diaries, 20/1/1879.
[4] Ibid, 8/1 & 12/1/1883.
[5] SDA179, Vaughan to Casartelli, 15/8/1883.
[6] Ibid, 19/8/1883.

> "In my own mind, I think you have been too apt to be satisfied with your own experience and that you have not sufficiently examined the experience of their places or sought for hints in the details of working other places, which are superior to St Bede's... you were perfectly satisfied with your own view on everything, whether this was fair or unfair, I do not say, but it is the impression you made, by your real ignorance. I suppose in what was being done elsewhere or by your manners always... I have no wish to diminish your authority as Prefect of Studies or to place you under another, but to secure for you those advantages which are still needed if the College is to attain the position you desire for it[1]".

Casartelli had had enough and asked for leave of absence from St Bede's and from the Diocese. This was granted and at the end of 1884 he returned to Louvain to study for his Doctorate in Oriental Languages[2]. Several months later Vaughan, maybe trying to make amends, wrote to him that "... At St Bede's they miss you a good deal[3]". He returned to Manchester for the 1885/86 academic year and slipped back into the Prefecture of Studies, but two months later, the college inspection by Dr Boardman[4] was to prove a further sticking point; the report criticised the teaching methods being undertaken at the College and on the 31st December, Casartelli wrote an angry letter attacking the conclusions:

> "I have hitherto always studiously refrained from making any demor or criticism upon your examination of our boys and your reports because I conceive that it is not my place, ordinarily, to do so, but rather to observe and profit by your observations. There are however, certain remarks and judgements in your last report and especially in your letter to His Lordship, which seem to make it my duty, in justice to the teaching staff, to express my conviction that these remarks and judgements are not as well founded as usual[5]".

Boardman's response was to stand by his conclusions and he went as far as to describe Casartelli's teaching methods as "trash"; he then sent on a copy of his letter and Casartelli's original to Vaughan, offering to resign as Examiner, if the Bishop felt his performance was found wanting[6]. In August 1885, Vaughan purchased the house on the North East corner of the College site, number 5 Mayfield Road, known as 'The Roost'. The property was bought from Mr Fox and was then rented out to the Casartelli family. Fr Casartelli now had his parents and sisters around the corner from

---

[1] SDA179, Vaughan to Casartelli, 25/7/1884.
[2] Broadley, J., 2006, Louis Charles Casartelli, Pg 30
[3] SDA179, Vaughan to Casartelli, 19/5/1885.
[4] The Rev Dr Charles Boardman DD (1831-1894) was Rector of St Wilfrid, Longridge and served as College Inspector.
[5] SBCA, Casartelli to Boardman, 31/12/1885.
[6] SBCA, Boardman to Vaughan, 1/1/1886.

the College and would frequent the house on a regular basis, recording regularly in his diaries that he saw the house as an escape from the stress of life in College.

Just over eighteen months after his dispute with Boardman, Casartelli recorded in his diary on the 15th September 1887 that he had resigned as Prefect of Studies, and then on the 19th that his resignation had been accepted; he offered to remain on the staff as a Professor and recommended to Vaughan that the post be offered to Fr Newton[1], late Prefect of Studies at Ushaw. Newton however declined the post and on the 21st, Casartelli made the following world-weary entry; "Hear that Fr. Newton has declined the post here, suppose I shall continue as before[2]". It was previously believed that when Casartelli withdrew his resignation, he then remained in the post until he became Rector in 1891. However, copies of the College Prospectus, recently rediscovered and covering the subsequent years, list Casartelli as 'Librarian and Museum Curator' and Mr Michael Sullivan as Prefect of Studies, so if he did indeed withdraw his resignation, then that withdrawal must have been rejected by Vaughan.

Sullivan himself in a memoir published in 1937 recalled this period: "He [Bishop Vaughan] wanted to make me Prefect of Studies. I accepted on condition of being given a free hand for two years. Then there was some change in the syllabus that took the Bishop's fancy, and he asked me to make the changes. I had to remind him of his promise, and he agreed to wait without any trouble[3]".

Some recollections of Fr Casartelli from his former students, during his time as Prefect of Studies were published in 1937 and present a different view to that of Vaughan and Boardman:

> "The Prefect of Studies was Fr L.C. Casartelli… I would like to refer to his wonderful way of imparting that knowledge to others… when I wanted to learn French, Spanish and Italian; he gave me a night each week in his bed-sitting room and made me write a letter to him weekly in the language under study, and he always returned that letter to me with corrections. No fee was ever mentioned, expected or paid – it was enough for him to encourage anyone desiring to share his knowledge…One Protestant friend admitted to me that he would rather spend an evening with Fr Casartelli than with anyone else in the world![4]". (HF O'Brien 1937)
>
> "It was a delight and pleasure to study under him. His teaching method was that of the University Professor… he did not believe in using exercise books; all that he insisted on was any clean piece of paper, legible writing and "sign your paper". After study these papers were taken to him, and at next morning's class

---

[1] Fr Henry Newton (1837-1902 – Ord. 1864) served on the staff at Ushaw until 1885, when he went on sick-leave. He succeeded Fr Joseph Wrennall as 14th Prefect of Studies there in 1869.

[2] UCA, Diary of Bishop Casartelli, 1877.

[3] BAEDA, New Series vol. 7.1, Easter 1937, p. 46.

[4] Ibid, new vol 12.1, Easter 1937, Pg7-8.

were distributed, with any corrections and suggestions in red ink[1]". (Fr H. Atkinson 1937)

"Dr Casartelli was a hero to me all the rest of my College days. Boys' hearts must be the most difficult to capture, but Dr Casartelli captured ours. His popularity with the boys was universal, and was well deserved[2]". (Fr Charles Wilkin 1937)

We also see in the mid-1880s a drastic reduction in staff levels with several long-standing and key Professors leaving the College. At the end of the 1885/86 academic year, Mr Lancelot Baugh left after five years and Fr John Vaughan resigned to join his brother in London at the House of Expiation. During the following academic year, 1886/87, Canon Hayes resigned as Vice-Rector and Fr Formby[3] as Professor, both due to ill-health, having served for seven and nine years respectively. Fr Bolton[4] also left, to go out on to the Mission. By 1888/89, there were only six clergy left on the teaching staff (including the Rector & Vice-Rector) and four laymen. If we look back to the 1883/84 academic year, there were nine clergy and six laymen, so the total professorial staff was reduced from fifteen to ten in six years.

Then we have the curious situation of Fr William Hill, who in 1877 was entrusted with the responsibility for keeping and maintaining the College Log Book / Diary and until 1881 he did this meticulously: Mr Sullivan later recalled that "whenever there was a concert or a prize-giving or a sports-day, there was no peace in the College until he was supplied with an official programme and the fullest of details[5]". But in 1881, for some unknown reason, the Log Book ceases. Ten years later, when Hill left the College staff, Casartelli as the new Rector contacted him and asked him to return the said Diary, to which Hill replied that he had "burnt it" and Casartelli begins a new Diary with the following entry:

"...The present entry prefixed to this bound volume of the New Series is made both to record and to solemnly protest against this unjustifiable detention and destruction of one of the most valuable possessions of the College[6]".

Thirty-nine years after this, Mgr Hill died in retirement at Salmesbury, and his sister with whom he had resided for some years, on sorting his personal effects, came across the missing Log Book and returned it to St Bede's[7]. He was probably embarrassed at having neglected his assigned duties for the past ten years, but the

---

[1] BAEDA, New Series vol. 7.1, Easter 1937, Pg 10-11.

[2] Ibid, p. 17.

[3] Fr Henry Formby (1850-1890 – Ord. 1878), was Minor Professor at Ushaw prior to coming to the College. He retired to Bury Convent in 1887 and died there three years later, aged only 40.

[4] Fr Thomas Bolton (1858-1907 – Ord. 1883) on staff 1883-87. Died as Rector of St Mary, Blackburn.

[5] BAEDA, new vol. 3.4, Jan 1930, p. 96.

[6] St Bede's College, Log Book, New Series vol. 1, 1891-1895.

[7] BAEDA, new vol. 3.4, Jan 1930, p. 96.

evidence also suggests some degree of bitterness, perhaps as a result of his ejection from the College, and yet despite this he donated the High Altar and Reredos for the new College Chapel in 1897[1].

At the end of the 1889/90 academic year, Vaughan finally conceded defeat and employed Fr Cornelius Pool[2] and Mr Gerald Keating BA as Classics Tutors[3], thus abandoning the purely Commercial School after only fifteen years, but it was too late and in the final year of existence, only fourteen new students enrolled at the College.

The Merger – 1891

Mgr de Clerc died suddenly on the 30th December 1889 and was replaced as Headmaster of the Salford Catholic Grammar School by Fr John Bromley Cooke[4]; the SCGS was by this stage oversubscribed and overcrowded, still existing as it did in the two converted houses on The Crescent, and by the late 1880s had an annual intake in excess of eighty boys on the registers (nearly twice that of St Bede's). The buildings were not only too small, but were also inadequate and unsuitable for modern educational purposes, and there was no room to expand.

At the same time St Bede's was entering its final crisis. New admissions were dropping; in 1886/87 the highest number was achieved, but even this was only twenty-seven in total, and in 1888/89 only twenty new pupils joined the College, and although 1889/90 would see a slight resurgence to twenty-four joiners, the final year of the College 1890/91 saw only fourteen; the College was shrinking rapidly and so, obviously, was the income.

In 1890, a Frenchman, Max LeClerc, visited the College as part of his research into the English educational system. His findings were published in 1894 in his book L'éducation et la Société en Angleterre and his conclusions on St Bede's were not complimentary:

> "St Bede's College, a commercial Catholic school, founded in 1876 by the Bishop of Salford, receives day pupils (12 guineas) and boarders (60 guineas). It is aimed at the leisured upper classes. Attractively situated next to a large park, on the edge of the elegant suburbs of the city, fitted with all the comforts of the public schools, it is directed by the secular clergy. The Catholic clergy have made the unusual decision, for a school founded by them and under their

---

[1] BAEDA, vol. 1.6, Easter 1898, p. 82.

[2] Canon Cornelius Pool (1857-1915 – Ord. 1884) 10th Prefect of Discipline 1890-91, died at St Joseph, Heywood.

[3] SBCA, St Bede's College Prospectus, 1890/92.

[4] Fr John Bromley Cooke (1859-1913 – ord. 1889), ended up as Rector at St Mary, Burnley. His nephew Mgr John Cuthbert Cooke VG (1890-1957 – ord. 1914) was also on the staff at St Bede's from 1917; he became 8th Prefect of Studies 1921; 12th Vice-Rector 1926 and 8th Rector in 1938. In 1950 he was appointed PP at St Edward's, Rusholme where he died.

direction, to exclude Greek as well as Latin: you will not find any trace of the two classical languages at St Bede's. The curriculum comprises modern languages, history, commercial geography, mathematics, physics and chemistry. The study of modern languages is the particular concern. In spite of all these advantages, and in spite of its low cost, St Bede's has not been entirely successful: it had fifty pupils on its roll in 1890. The Bishop of Salford was clearly deceiving himself when he thought that a commercial school for the use of the leisured classes would be a success in Manchester. True, there are 110,000 Catholics in this city, but almost all are poor and the few rich families prefer to give their children a classical education[1]".

What is clear is that by the start of the 1890s, Vaughan had two main problems; both St Bede's and the Pastoral Seminary were 'dead in the water' while the SCGS, although institutionally successful, was at breaking point. His solution was a stroke of genius: he would bring the SCGS to Alexandra Park and into the buildings of St Bede's. The Classical College and Junior Seminary would then have the benefits of the healthy spacious surroundings and well-equipped facilities; the Commercial College could survive, albeit reduced to a mere department of the larger institution and with the Diocesan Clergy being trained together on site, with the Bishop also in residence, he could then fufil some of the aims of the Seminary of Pastoral Theology as well.

Mgr Wrennall resigned at the end of the 1890/91 academic year; he was by then in his late 60s and his health was beginning to decline. Vaughan appointed Casartelli as the Rector of the combined school; he was felt to be a good compromise candidate as a former pupil of the SCGS and longstanding Master at St Bede's, and presumably he and the Bishop had reconciled since their falling out in 1887. Wrennall then took the post of Procurator, Fr Cooke became Vice-Rector & Prefect of Studies and Fr Francis Hart[2] Prefect of Discipline. Mgr Gadd, Fr Hill and Fr Pool all left the College.

In September 1891 the new combined school opened and during the first month, a total of 131 pupils enrolled; 64 were former Grammar School pupils; 38 remained from the Commercial College; 4 came from St Chad's High and the remaining 25 were previously unattached[3]. Clearly the SCGS pupils who made up 49% of the new College outnumbered the ex-Bedians who comprised only 29% of the new school.

---

[1] LeClerc, M., 1894, *L'education et la société en Angleterre*.

[2] Fr Francis J. Hart (1859-1915 – Ord. 1891) sent immediately to St Bede's; 11th Prefect of Discipline 1891-92; 2nd Procurator 1894-99; 5th Vice-Rector 1896-1900. Went to St John the Baptist, Padiham in 1902 as Rector where he died.

[3] St Bede's College, Admission Registers, vol. 2, 1891-1905.

The Main College Building, as it would have looked upon completion. This was the design drawn by Ernest Bower-Norris in 1924.

The College from Alexandra Park, circa 1880. The South Wing has been finished but the Central Block is yet to be built and the front of the Aquarium Hall is still visible. The house on the far left of the picture is Ebenezer House, with Hampton Grange between it and the College. The empty plot between the two houses would later be occupied by the Cenacle Convent St Regis Retreat House.

Canon James Hayes
2nd Vice-Rector 1877-1886
In residence 1886-1890

Bishop Louis Charles Casartelli
1st Prefect of Studies 1877-1887
3rd Rector 1891-1903
4th Bishop of Salford 1903-1925

Monsignor Charles Gadd
3rd Vice-Rector 1886-1891

The Academic Hall, laid out as the church. Circa 1885

The Senior Dormitory. Circa 1895

Mr Edward Pyke
Head of Modern Languages 1885-1926
9th Prefect of Discipline 1886-1890

Mr Michael A. Sullivan
Head of Mathematics 1879-1926
2nd Prefect of Studies 1887-1891

Mr John J. Cardwell
Head of Geography 1884-1922

The Main Corridor Circa 1895.

The Commercial Museum located in the Chapel Corridor. This area is now occupied by the Maher Library foyer, reception and IT Room.

The first College Pavilion, located on the original Cricket Field on College Road.
Circa 1895.

The College Refectory in the extension at the rear of Hampton Grange. Circa 1915.

CONCLUSION

So what can we conclude about the sixteen-year existence of the St Bede's Commercial College? Certainly the school was not a success, at least not to the extent that Snead-Cox claimed when he stated that it was "flourishing" at the time of the 1891 merger; in fact by this point the College was actually 'on its last legs', Vaughan's Commercial Dream had effectively failed and the St Bede's College that went onward from 1891 would be more the Salford Catholic Grammar School under an assumed name than it was a continuation of the 1876 foundation. The primary and most severe issue was clearly the inability to attract sufficient students; the Catholic Middle Class parents of Manchester were not taken with the concept. Now this is not to say that the parents were opposed to the idea of giving their sons a Commercial Education, but what they were opposed to was the idea of denying their sons a Classical Education; after all, the legal and medical professions still at that stage required a knowledge of Latin and Greek, not to mention the requirements for a knowledge of the two languages within the Catholic Church, and thus by choosing to exclude them from the syllabus, Vaughan arguably committed his biggest mistake and alienated a large percentage of his potential customers. Max LeClerc was quite clear where he placed the blame for the failure, stating that "Bishop Vaughan was deceiving himself" and basically concluding that the College was institutionally flawed.

The inability of the school to attract and retain its students meant that as a financial business the Commercial College was never sustainable; they were never at full capacity, but despite this a full staff still had to be employed in order to maintain the full curriculum, and thus there were large financial losses each year. We must not however write off the College as an absolute failure; despite its short existence and small number of alumni, Old-Bedians populated the Empire, making their names in business, in banking, in politics and in the military. The College produced world leaders and many of these chose to retain a relationship with their alma mater for the remainder of their lives.

If we examine the role played by the managing triumvirate of the College, we have three very different men; Herbert Vaughan was the ideas man, but also the financier; Mgr Wrennall was the practical no-nonsense administrator and Fr Casartelli was the academic brain; relations between the three were, as we have seen, not always cordial.

Herbert Vaughan's role in the whole affair is probably the most complex; at times he appears to be three different men; there is the Herbert Vaughan who was the College Founder, who had conceived of the idea in 1872 and was anxious to get started; then there was the Herbert Vaughan who was at war with the Jesuits and for whom St Bede's became little more than a pawn in the chess game; and finally there was the Herbert Vaughan who was College Director and who was determined to make the school work at any costs; the three personas were often in conflict with each other and caused conflict with the other staff. Vaughan was almost certainly a dreamer: he conceived ideas that nobody else would have considered and while sometimes those ideas worked, more often than not they didn't. If we had to identify the greatest flaw in the Bishop's personality, it would be his self-assuredness; he had almost a belief in his own infallibility and consequently when he conceived one of his schemes, instead of seeking counsel or gaining the opinion of his advisors as Turner would have done, Vaughan instead announced the plan as a fait accompli, always on the premise that his ideas must automatically be great ones. There was no democracy under Vaughan's leadership. When the Covered Playground was being built, he believed he could be an architect – and almost caused a disaster in the process; when he decided to spread St Bede's into Europe, he launched his plans without ever asking the parents at the College, how many of them would actually be interested in sending their sons to Germany, and when very few were, he blamed the parents for their 'apathy'. This was an example of another character trait of Vaughan, which was that when his plans failed to work out, he always found somebody else to blame: in 1877 it was Fr Wood; in 1881 it was Mgr Wrennall and then in 1884 it was Fr Casartelli.

Casartelli meanwhile, in my opinion comes across as being somewhat temperamental. He was initially unhappy at the College and didn't want to stay; he fell out with Vaughan, requested leave of absence to return to Louvain, fell out with Dr Boardman and then resigned from his post. His success as Prefect of Studies is debatable: there is no doubt that he was a brilliant academic, but was he a good High Schoolmaster? Clearly Vaughan and Boardman held these abilities in very low esteem and both criticise him for his methods, but he seems to have been reasonably popular with the students.

It is the Rector however, Mgr Wrennall, who comes across to me as the most likeable character of the three; practical, clear headed and no nonsense, he was the administrator who managed the day-to-day running of St Bede's, appearing sometimes to be piggy-in-the-middle between the constantly changing whims of his Bishop and the temperamental behaviour of his Prefect of Studies, and he just seems to take whatever is thrown at him and gets on with it.

What the three men have in common however is that in their own ways they each cared deeply about St Bede's and devoted their lives to trying to make it work; so much so that Vaughan moved into the College Lodge, so he could be on site, and he also expended vast fortunes on the place; when Wrennall retired from active service, he too took up residence in the Lodge and remained there until his death, still involved in the College and in the affairs of the boys. After Wrennall's death, Casartelli, by then Bishop of Salford, moved into the Lodge and also remained onsite at the College until his death, and made it his dying wish to see the main building completed. So although they may have disagreed over the minutiae, each had the welfare of the school close to his heart.

Overall the history of the St Bede's Commercial College was in many ways a 'Comedy of Errors'. The first eighteen months were akin to a theatrical performance, from the purchase of the non-existent land and the faux opening and announcement, to the actual premature opening, probably instigated by the impending visit of Cardinal Franchi. Under Wrennall a more serious approach was taken, but interspersed by Vaughan's purchase of the aquarium and subsequent attempts to run the same, resulting in exhibits eating each other and the escaped alligator running loose in the Academic Hall, the expense frivolously incurred in the construction of the totally impractical College building, the almost catastrophic construction of the Covered Playground and not least the failed German experiment, where not only did they try to launch the new school on a public holiday, but failed to seek Government permission to open it at all - the situations are almost humorous and it would be the 1894 exposé of the financial affairs of the College that would prove the watershed for St Bede's and would be instrumental in putting the past behind them and in preparing the school for its bright future.

BIBLIOGRAPHY

ANON, *St Patrick's RC Club Jubilee Souvenir Book*, (Manchester, 1927)
BOLTON, Rev Charles, *Salford Diocese & its Catholic Past* (Manchester, 1950)
BROADLEY, Rev. Dr Martin John, *Bishop Vaughan & the Jesuits* (Suffolk, 2010)
BROADLEY, Rev. Dr Martin John, *Louis Charles Casartelli* (Bury, 2006)
CROFT & GILLOW, *Historical Account of Lisbon College* (Barnet, 1902)
DEVADDER CFX, Jan, *The Life and Times of TJ Ryken*, (Bruges, 1986)
LANNON, Rev. Dr David, *Catholic Education in the Salford Diocese*, (Unpublished PhD Thesis, University of Hull, 2003)
LANNON, Rev. Dr David, *Educational Provision within the Salford Diocesan Area*, (Unpublished M.Phil Thesis, University of Hull, 1994)
LE CLERC, Max, *L'education et la société en Angleterre* (1894)
LESLIE, Shane, *Letters of Cardinal Vaughan to Lady Herbert of Lea* (London, 1948)
McCORMACK, Arthur, *Cardinal Vaughan* (London, 1966)
MILBURN, David, *A History of Ushaw College* (Durham, 1964)
O'DEA, John, *The Story of the Old Faith in Manchester* (London, 1910)
O'NEILL MHM, Robert, *Cardinal Herbert Vaughan* (Tunbridge Wells, 1995)
ROBERTS, I.D. *Jesuit Collegiate Education in England*, (Durham, 1986)
SNEAD-COX, John, *Life of Cardinal Vaughan*, 2 Volumes (London, 1910)
WILSON, John Marius, *Imperial Gazetteer of England & Wales*, (Edinburgh, 1870)

Magazines, Newspapers & Periodicals

Baeda, (Magazine of St Bede's College)
Catholic Directory of England & Wales
The Harvest (Magazine of the Salford Diocese)
Manchester Guardian Newspaper
NW Catholic History Journal
Recusant History Journal
Salford Diocesan Almanac
St Bede's Gazette
St Bede's Magazine
The Edmundian, (Magazine of St Edmund's Ware)
The Tablet Newspaper
Frondes Silvulae, (Magazine of the Salford Catholic Grammar School)

ABREVIATIONS

Bart.	Baronet
Br.	Brother
CFX	Congregation of Francis Xavier / Xaverian
CSSR	Congregation of the Most Holy Redeemer / Redemptorist
DD	Doctor of Divinity
Dr	Doctor
Fr	Reverend Father
Jnr	Junior
Lt	Lieutenant
MA	Master of the Arts
Mgr	Monsignor
MHM	Mill Hill Missionary
MLitt	Master of Letters
OP	Order of Preachers / Dominican
OSB	Order of St Benedict / Benedictine
OSF	Order of St Francis / Franciscan
OSFC	Order of Friars Minor Capuchin
PhD	Doctor of Philosophy
RC	Roman Catholic
Rev	Reverend
RN	Royal Navy
SBC	St Bede's College
SBCA	St Bede's College Archives
SCGS	Salford Catholic Grammar School
SDA	Salford Diocesan Archives
SDA CD	Salford Diocesan Archives, Compact Disc
SJ	Society of Jesus / Jesuit
Snr	Senior
St	Saint
UCA	Ushaw College Archives
Vol	Volume

Appendix 1 – St Bede's College Management

Rectors

1876-1877 Fr Charles Walter Wood
1877-1891 Mgr Thomas Wrennall
1891-1903 Fr Dr Louis Charles Casartelli DD DLitt Or MA
1903-1912 Fr Dr Anselm Poock DD
1912-1915 Bishop Dr John Vaughan DD
1915-1916 Fr James Cartin
1916-1938 Mgr Francis Gonne MA
1938-1950 Mgr John Cuthbert Cooke MA
1950-1966 Mgr Dr Thomas Duggan PhD MA
1966-1967 Fr Geoffrey Burke MA
1967-1974 Mgr Eric Riley MA
1974-2008 Mgr Terence Dodgeon MA
2008 Position Abolished

Vice-Rectors

1876-1877 Fr James Moyes
1877-1885 Fr James Hayes
1885-1891 Mgr Charles Joseph Gadd
1891-1896 Fr John Bromley Cooke
1896-1900 Fr Francis J. Hart
1900-1905 Fr John Thomas Bousfield
1905-1912 Fr Dr Thomas Henshaw DD
1912-1915 Fr James Cartin
1915-1916 Fr William J. Hughes BD BA
1917-1922 Fr Arthur Joseph Wilson *Died in office*
1922-1925 Fr Joseph Lomax
1925-1938 Fr John Cuthbert Cooke MA
1938-1950 Fr Leo Charles Knowles MA
1950-1951 Fr Dr Francis J. Shutt DD PhD BCC MA
1951-1953 Fr T. Bernard McClernon
1953-1966 Fr Geoffrey Burke MA
1966-1970 Fr John Groarke STL MA
1970-1974 Fr Terence Dodgeon MA
1974-1998 Fr Bernard Noel Jackson
1998 Position Abolished

Procurators / Bursars

1891-1894 Mgr Thomas Wrennall
1894-1899 Fr Francis J. Hart *(also Vice-Rector)*
1899-1900 Fr James Higgins
1900-1912 Fr Dr Anselm Poock *(also Rector)*
1912-1922 Fr Arthur Joseph Wilson *(also Vice-Rector)*
1922-1926 Fr George G. Wainwright
1926-1932 Fr Charles Wilkin
1932-1937 Fr Francis Joseph Lynch
1937-1946 Fr T. Bernard McClernon
1946-1985 Fr Bernard Noel Jackson *(also Vice-Rector)*
1985-1986 Mr Austin Whittam *(Died in post)*
1986-1991 Mr David Holland
1991-2010 Mr Leo Fletcher

Prefects of Studies

1877-1887 Fr Dr Louis Charles Casartelli DD DLitt Or MA
1887-1891 Mr Michael A. Sullivan
1891-1894 Fr John Bromley Cooke *(also Vice-Rector)*
1904-1905 Fr John Thomas Bousfield (*also Vice-Rector)*
1905-1909 Fr Peter Higgins
1909-1913 Fr James Cartin
1913-1918 Fr Francis Gonne MA *(also Rector)*
1918-1921 Fr John Francis McNulty MA
1921-1938 Fr John Cuthbert Cooke MA *(also Vice-Rector)*
1938-1950 Fr Charles Leo Knowles MA *(also Vice-Rector)*
1950-1966 Fr Geoffrey Burke MA (*also Vice-Rector)*
1966-1974 Mr Vincent Ganley
1974-1989 Mgr Terence Dodgeon MA *(also Rector)*
1989 Position Abolished

Prefects of Discipline

1877-1877 Fr William L. Fowler
1877-1878 Fr William Hill
1878-1879 Fr Charles Murray Browne
1879-1880 Fr Joseph Crilly
1880-1880 Fr Patrick Nowlan *(died in post)*
1880-1881 Fr Patrick J. Mann
1881-1884 Fr Thomas Corbishley
1884-1886 Mr Lancelot L. Baugh
1886-1890 Mr Edward Pyke
1890-1891 Fr Cornelius W. Pool
1891-1892 Fr Francis J. Hart
1892-1894 Fr Francis Oakes
1894-1898 Fr John Manning
1898-1900 Fr James Morris
1900-1901 Fr George Cobb
1901-1902 Fr Joseph Bannon
1902-1905 Fr James Cartin
1905-1909 Fr Arthur Joseph Wilson
1909-1915 Fr Robert McGuinness
1915-1915 Fr Victor Mann
1915-1922 Fr John Francis McNulty MA
1922-1925 Fr James B. McGinnell
1925-1925 Fr Hugh O'Neill
1925-1928 Fr Leo Charles Knowles MA
1928-1931 Fr George Catterall
1931-1932 Fr Francis Joseph Lynch
1932-1932 Fr T. Bernard McClernon
1932-1935 Fr Dr Walter Dempsey PhD
1935-1937 Fr. Arthur O'Connor Jnr.
1937-1942 Fr Ignatius Knowles
1942-1946 Fr Joseph Cain
1946-1949 Fr James Dwyer
1949-1950 Fr William Lindon
1950-1955 Fr Peter Pessagno
1955-1958 Fr John Rigby
1958-1962 Fr Anthony Lawton
1962-1966 Fr Anthony Grimshaw
1966-1969 Fr Robert Livesey
1969-1971 Fr David Haley
1971-1977 Fr John Neville
1977-1980 Fr Peter Wilkinson
1980-1990 Mr Joseph Shaw
1990 Position Abolished

Appendix 2 – Commercial College Captains (Head Boys)

1877/78
Michaelmas – James Mahoney
Lent – Ernest Annacker
Easter – Thomas Flavin

1878/79
Michaelmas – Ernest Annacker
Lent – Joseph Donohoe
Easter – Thomas Flavin

1879/80
Michaelmas – Joseph Donohoe
Lent – George C. Mesnard
& Edward J. Wall
Easter – Joseph Donohoe

1880/81
Michaelmas – Edward Wall
Lent – John L. O'Neill
Easter – Charles J. Farrington

1882/83
Michaelmas – Walter J. Hennessy
Lent – Peter Graham
Easter – John McMullan

1883/84
Michaelmas – Peter Graham
Epiphany – Joseph Cullinan
Easter – Albert La Montague

1884/85
Michaelmas – Antrum Allen
Epiphany – John O'Neill
Easter – Gilbert A. Graham

1885/86
Michaelmas – Wilfrid J. Carter
& Charles O'Callaghan
Epiphany – Thomas M. Walsh
Easter – Michael Hughes

1886/87
Michaelmas – Owen Comerford
& Michael Hughes
Epiphany – Edward Meagher
Easter – Ernest Winter

1887/88
Michaelmas – Wm McDonnell
Epiphany – Thomas M. Eastman
Easter – Charles H. Boone

1888/89
Michaelmas – Alberto C. Lima
& Robert A. Swarbrick
Epiphany – Charles H. Byrne
Easter – Chares Burgoyne

1889/90
Michaelmas – Ramon Mandisla
Epiphany – Charles Burgoyne
Easter – Frank Gransaull

1890/91
Michaelmas – Leon Burgoyne
Epiphany – Frank Gransaull
Easter - Robert Rooney

Appendix 3 – Map of Alexandra Park, circa 1900

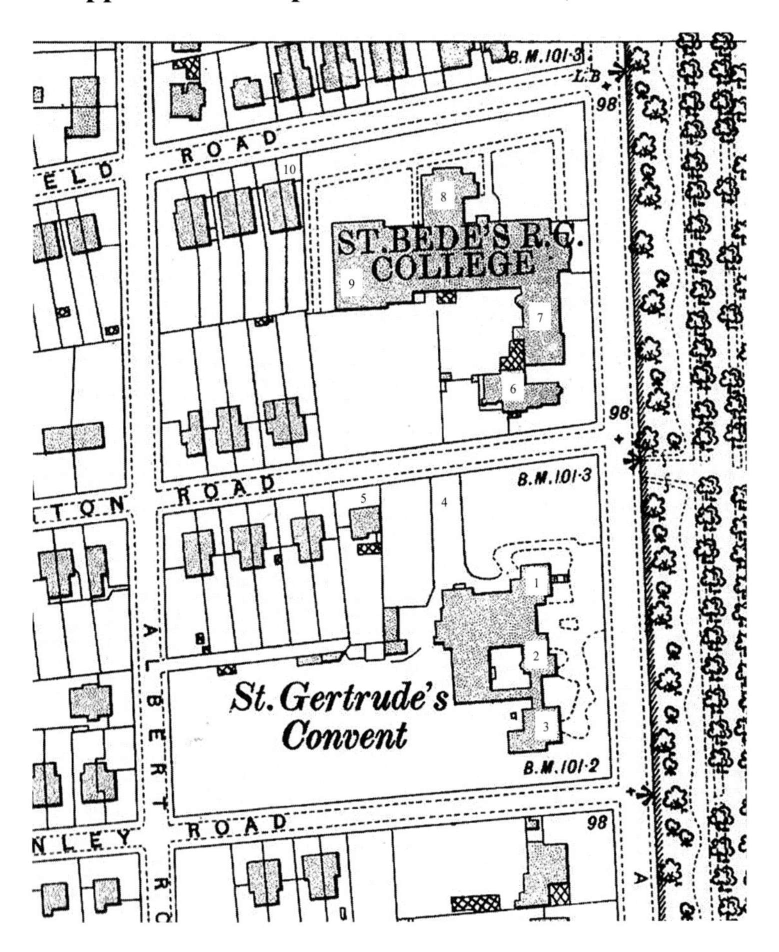

The Cenacle Convent has been built incorporating Ebenezer House (1) and Rose Lawn (2) and connecting via a passage into Avon Lodge (3). The Regis Retreat House however has not yet been constructed and its site (4) is still gardens.

Both Mayfield and Wellington Roads are still lined with houses; these would later be demolished as the College expanded, with exception to Holly Bank (5).

On the north-side of Wellington Road, Hampton Grange (6) has been extended and incorporated into the new building (7), the new chapel (8) has also been constructed on the side of the former aquarium hall, while at the rear can be seen the covered playground (9). Number (10) is 'The Roost', home of the Casartelli family.

Appendix 4 – Map of Grosvenor Square, Circa 1860

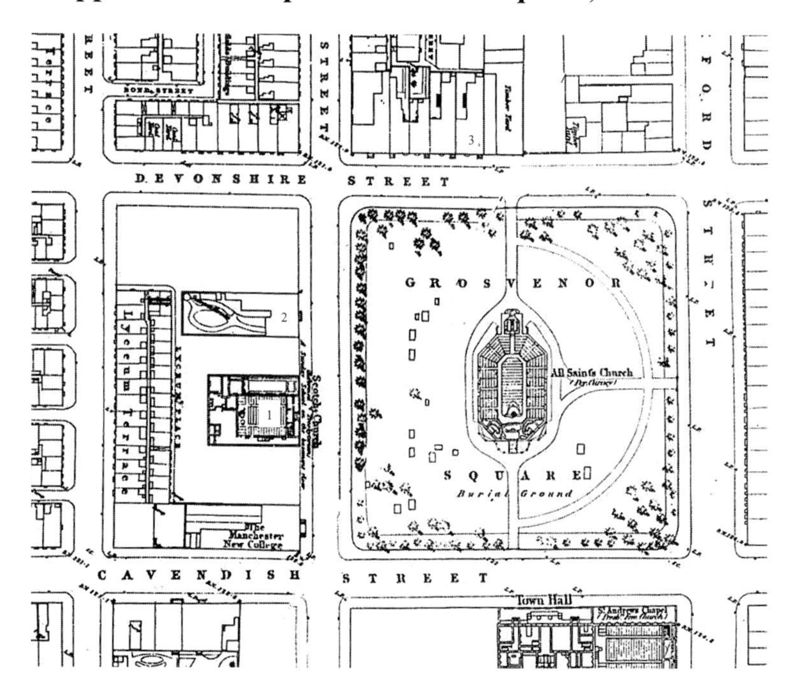

The building (1) on the left hand side of the square, labelled 'Scotch Church', is the chapel which would later become St Alphonsus and then The Holy Family; the site is today occupied by St Augustine's RC Church. The building above it (2) is the house later occupied by the Catholic Collegiate Institute.

On the Devonshire Street side of the square, the first base of St Bede's College was in the house (3) alongside the larger of the two blocks labelled 'Timber Yard'.

Appendix 5 – List of College Founders

Herbert, Cardinal Vaughan

Henry, 14th Duke of Norfolk

Sir Humphrey de Trafford, Bart

The Marchesse Murphy

Abbot Sir David Hunter-Blair, Bart

Mr Lawrence O'Neill Esq.

The Right Reverend Mgr James Lennon

The Right Reverend Mgr John Canon Kershaw

Mr Richard Holden K.S.G.

The Right Reverend Mgr John Canon Burke

Sir Edward Hulton, Bart

Appendix 6 – List of Leaders of the Annual College Retreat

1880 – Rev. Fr Plunkett CSSR

1881- Rev. Fr Bridgett CSSR

1882 – Rev. Fr H. Morgan CSSR

1883 – Rev. Fr H. Morgan CSSR

1884 – Right Rev. Mgr F. Weld

1885 – Rev. Fr Bernard Vaughan SJ

1886 – Rev. Fr W.H. Anderson SJ

1887 – Rev. Fr Pius Cavanagh OP

1888 – Rev. Fr Charles W. Wood

1889 – Rev. Fr Bernard Vaughan SJ

1890 – Rev. Fr G. Seadon CRP

1891 – Rev. Fr George Richardson

Appendix 7 – List of winners of Annual College Prizes

The Rectors Prize for Good Conduct & Diligence

1877 – James Mahoney
1878 – James Rowntree
1879 – James Rowntree
1880 – Alfred Gilbertson
1881 – Charles Farrington
1882 – Alejandro de Bango
1883 – William Barker
1884 – Richard Farrington
1885 – Carlos Gomez
1886 – Emilio de Arana

Essay Prize

1882 – John A. McMullan
1883 – Edward Hulton
1884 – Joseph Alton
1885 – Edward Julton
1887 – Edward Meagher
1888 – William McElligott

Athletic Sports

1878 – Thomas Banks
1879 – Bernard B. Hughes
1881 – John Hubbertsey
1882 – Albert La Montague
1883 – Albert La Montague
1884 – Albert La Montague
1885 – Charles O'Callaghan

Cricket High Score

1879 – Thomas Flavin (49)
1880 – Daniel McCann (46)
1881 – John Farrington (47)
1882 – John Gornall (53)
1883 – John Farrington (71)
1884 – Peter Graham (31)
1885 – Richard Farrington (106)

Mental Arithmetic Prize

1884 – John Meagher & Antrum Allen
1885 – Edward Meagher & John O'Neill
1886 – Ambrose Ashworth & Frederick Nicholson
1887 – Frederick Nicholson, Charles Burgoyne & Vincent Hicks
1888 – Francis Ashworth & William Finnigan
1889 – William Finnigan & John Adamson
1890 – Herbert Kelly & William Finigan

Modern Languages Prize

1885 – Michael Hughes (French)
1888 – Ambrose Ashworth (French, German, Spannish & Italian)

INDEX

Back Cover – Cardinal Vaughan pictured with the staff and boys of St Bede's on the Rhine in 1891